"In *The Polyvagal Theory Workbook for Trauma*, Arielle Schwartz gives you practical, embodied tools along with compassionate guidance to support your healing journey. She makes the complexity of trauma recovery understandable and accessible while creating a wellspring of hope. Her warmth and kindness shine through her words."

—**Peter A. Levine, PhD**, developer of Somatic Experiencing; and author of several books, including *Waking the Tiger* and *In an Unspoken Voice*

"Arielle Schwartz has written an immensely practical guide that makes trauma integration accessible for everyone. A masterful somatic teacher, she invites the reader into a step-by-step approach to recovering resilience and well-being. This could not come at a more critical time when we all need helpful tools that settle and ground our daily challenges into manageable experiences."

—**Manuela Mischke-Reeds, MFT**, somatic trauma therapist, author of *Somatic Psychotherapy Toolbox*, and a founder of Hakomi Institute of California and Embodywise

"Arielle Schwartz has masterfully brought you another workbook that balances the seriousness of traumatizing experiences while providing practical tools that support healing without having to relive your past. She translates complex neuroscience into understandable and relatable language that can be easily applied into your life. She has the capacity to address the depth of pain that accompanies relational wounds while bringing a sense of hope that you can reclaim your birthright of connection to yourself, others, and the world around you. I highly recommend this book to all seeking a compassionate guide to trauma recovery."

—**Diane Poole Heller, PhD**, author of *The Power of Attachment*, and expert in the fields of trauma resolution and adult attachment theory

"Arielle Schwartz's clear and thoughtful writing illuminates our body's wisdom and capacity to ground, balance, heal, nourish, and restore our own well-being. *The Polyvagal Theory Workbook for Trauma* is an ally for the challenging times we are living in. Being embodied in a trauma-informed way is a powerful practice and necessary skill when human rights are threatened. With Arielle's guidance, readers can access their innate resilience and capacity to live as fully and presently as possible."

> —**Amber Elizabeth Gray, PhD**, Amber Gray Moving Therapies,
> human rights psychotherapist, and creator of Polyvagal-informed somatic
> and dance/movement therapy

"As a physician studying how the body holds trauma, I'm deeply impressed by Schwartz's ability to bridge science and physiology with accessible healing strategies. She guides us into our inner world with wisdom and compassion, helping us create lasting change in our nervous system. This workbook is a vital resource for redirecting our physiology toward health and connection."

> —**Aimie Apigian, MD, MS, MPH**, board-certified addiction and preventive
> medicine physician, and author of *The Biology of Trauma*

"This guide reveals the profound role our nervous system plays in both saving us, and helping us heal love and safety. Get ready for 'breathing, being weighted, and shaking it' out to have a whole new meaning."

> —**Staci K. Haines**, author of *The Politics of Trauma*

"Schwartz's groundbreaking work shows us that peak performance starts with a regulated nervous system. By blending polyvagal science with accessible somatic practices, this workbook offers high performers a compassionate, powerful path to both optimal resilience and deeper connection—proving that when we feel safe in our bodies, we unlock our greatest potential."

> —**Mastin Kipp**, cocreator of Functional Life Coaching, and author of
> *Claim Your Power* and *Reclaim Your Nervous System*

The
Polyvagal
Theory
Workbook
for Trauma

Body-Based Activities to
Regulate, Rebalance, and
Rewire Your Nervous System
Without Reliving the Trauma

Arielle Schwartz, PhD

New Harbinger Publications, Inc.

Publisher's Note

This publication is designed to provide accurate and authoritative information in regard to the subject matter covered. It is sold with the understanding that the publisher is not engaged in rendering psychological, financial, legal, or other professional services. If expert assistance or counseling is needed, the services of a competent professional should be sought.

NEW HARBINGER PUBLICATIONS is a registered trademark of New Harbinger Publications, Inc.

New Harbinger Publications is an employee-owned company.

Copyright © 2025 by Arielle Schwartz
New Harbinger Publications, Inc.
5720 Shattuck Avenue
Oakland, CA 94609
www.newharbinger.com

Cover design by Amy Shoup

Acquired by Jed Bickman

Edited by M. C. Calvi

Library of Congress Cataloging-in-Publication Data on file

Printed in the United States of America

27   26   25

10   9   8   7   6   5   4   3   2   1   First Printing

*To all who engage in the courageous journey of healing from trauma,
may this path guide you home to the compassionate heart
of your wisest Self.*

Contents

Foreword

Dear Reader,

Like almost everything in my life, I came to my understanding of how trauma is held in the body through my own direct experience. I learned to sit with searingly uncomfortable experiences with self-awareness. Even though my instinct was to pretend, to deny, to wish it wasn't so, to avoid, I chose to move toward the discomfort through my daily practice, through self-study and through gathering as much knowledge as possible on the topic of trauma and the body. Like many of you who are reading this book, I found self-psychoeducation both empowering and liberating. It helped me to make sense of myself and of my life. And without the powerful practices of meditation and yoga, my traumatized and neurodivergent nervous system would not have had the integrative capacity to metabolize all the information that I was learning.

About this discomfort, my Ashtanga teacher, Prem Carlisi, would say to me: "The Yoga is in what you choose to do next."

Years later, I began studying with Bessel van der Kolk, and then training in all the modalities that he suggested. Without the tempering of nervous system and the steadying of the mind through embodied practices, I doubt that I would have been able to move toward the hidden wounds of my inner child, nor the collective traumatization of my family and the historical traumatization of my peoples. None of this healing, for me, came from talk therapy. Rather, it came from approaches that require *some* capacity for embodiment and embodied discomfort.

And yet, before all of this, even before meditation and yoga, my healing journey began with stable, affordable housing nestled in a black spruce forest on the subarctic tundra of interior Alaska. Safety. Relative safety. Enough safety to begin the uncomfortable work of healing.

We cannot and will not achieve liberation, individually or collectively, without some discomfort. And yet, for many trauma survivors, being uncomfortable has become intertwined with being unsafe, being threatened, being in danger, or being in pain. As such, our threat detection system signals alarm at the slightest whiff of discomfort.

Befriending the nervous system allows us to develop enough mastery in order to experience *enough safety* in order to *discern the difference* between the discomfort that will grow us and the discomfort that leads to further pain and constriction.

Moving toward discomfort, tethered to relative safety, in baby steps, is the path to this discernment—and the path to personal freedom from the legacy of trauma. Oopsies and ouchies will happen along the way as you start to apply what you are learning. This is a natural part of the learning process. This is how we get to know ourselves and our nervous systems. Please don't let this dampen your innate desire to learn, to grow, and to thrive.

This book is a valuable resource and foundation for healing. In these pages, Arielle skillfully translates personal experiences and professional expertise into approachable education, concrete skills, and compassionate question prompts.

When I first met Arielle in October 2022, I was immediately struck by her authenticity and genuine dedication to embodying the practices and teachings she shares with others. Her writing is a reflection of her extensive knowledge and the wisdom teachings that have defined her own journey. Infused with kindness, wisdom, and a steadfast commitment to a better world, Arielle gently guides us through a process of self-discovery and empowerment, revealing the healing potential that lies within each of us.

I truly hope her work resonates with you, providing meaningful guidance as you navigate your own path toward self-education, personal growth, and wholeness. *The Polyvagal Theory Workbook for Trauma* stands as a sincere and down-to-earth contribution to fostering a compassionate and connected world.

I have no doubt that this book will help you make sense of yourself and your life.

With unwavering encouragement and a joyful commitment to discomfort as the path to personal freedom and collective liberation,

—Linda Thai, LMSW, ERYT-200
Thái Kim Ngọc 蔡金玉
Trauma therapist. Educator. Former child refugee.
Happy human being.

Introduction

Choosing to read a book focused on trauma recovery is itself an act of courage. Whether you have faced a single traumatic incident, are recovering from the effects of ongoing or repeated difficult life events, or are impacted by the distress of collective losses we are facing in our world, this book is for you. I know that the impact of trauma is profoundly painful. You may feel as though your life has been derailed, and if you grew up with trauma in your childhood home, you might feel as though you never got on the right track in the first place. It is important to know that there is a path forward and that you can still live a meaningful, enjoyable, and satisfying life.

The symptoms of adverse life events are as much in the body as they are in the mind. The shock of traumatic events can leave you feeling shaky, nauseous, or dizzy. Emotionally, you might experience terror, rage, shame, and despair. The ongoing repercussions of these events can leave you feeling restless, irritable, and vigilant of your surroundings, making it difficult to relax or sleep at night. Or, you might feel fatigued and lack the energy you need to face the day. These symptoms are the result of imbalances in your autonomic nervous system which is your body's built-in stress response system.

Treatment for trauma typically involves reviewing and reflecting on memories of traumatic events. Such interventions for trauma recovery focus on the stories of your losses while attending to the mental and emotional repercussions. Unfortunately, those traditional approaches are often triggering and can lead you to feel retraumatized. They also assume that the traumatic events are over; however, in our modern world, we are often navigating the ongoing exposure to threats that we see in our daily lives or in the media. Therefore, this workbook is designed to help you attend to your symptoms without reliving or overfocusing on your pain. Rather than focusing on the stories of your past, you will learn the tools to help you with the physiological effects of traumatic stress through the applied the science of *polyvagal theory*, also known as "the science of safety." In these pages, you will discover interventions that you can integrate into your life on a daily basis that will help you connect to yourself with greater ease and self-compassion. You will discover gentle breathing, movement, and body awareness practices that will help you attend to discomfort without feeling overwhelmed.

Polyvagal theory recognizes that your *vagus nerve* is a key to mind-body health. The vagus nerve is considered to be a superhighway of communication between your brain and your body. The word "vagus" is Latin for "wandering." This is an appropriate descriptor because this key nerve in your body connects your brain to your stomach, intestines, heart, lungs, throat, ears, and facial muscles. By applying polyvagal theory to trauma treatment, you can rebalance your nervous system, and as a result, the mental and emotional repercussions of trauma become more manageable. Through the lens of polyvagal theory, this workbook will give you practical tools to help you feel resourced for the journey of trauma recovery.

What Is Polyvagal Theory?

Your autonomic nervous system consists of two subsystems: the sympathetic and parasympathetic nervous systems. The sympathetic nervous system helps you meet the demands of stressful events by allowing you to mobilize your body for the purpose of self-protection. This is often referred to as the fight-or-flight response. The parasympathetic nervous system is often thought to be a recovery system that helps you rest in stillness, digest your food, and restore all of your bodily systems. This is often referred to as the relaxation response. When functioning well, your autonomic nervous system helps you rise up to meet the challenges of everyday stressors and also allows you to recover quickly and efficiently. When out of balance, you might feel trapped between experiences of being keyed up in anxiety or shut down with exhaustion. Simply put, you become less resilient to stress. Moreover, when the nervous system is dysregulated, you are more likely to have difficulties with other systems in your body, which can lead to blood pressure changes, blood sugar imbalances, digestive disturbances, asthma, and auto-immune conditions.

The vagus nerve always engages the parasympathetic nervous system. "Poly" in Greek is translated as "many," and in this context, polyvagal theory proposes that we have two branches of the vagus nerve. Polyvagal theory was originated by Dr. Stephen Porges, after he observed an unexpected paradox in relationship to the parasympathetic nervous system. When you are in a safe context, you are able access your relaxation response through a branch of the vagus nerve called the myelinated ventral vagal complex (myelin is a fatty coating that strengthens a nerve pathway through repeated practice). However, when you are experiencing a threat, there is an evolutionary older branch of the vagus nerve called the dorsal vagal complex that protects you by withdrawing, hiding, becoming smaller, and becoming still in order to avoid being detected by a potential predator. In some cases, this can lead to a "feigned death" response in which you faint. This protective response is more likely to occur when you have faced a threatening experience in which there is no exit—whether because there is no way to escape or because the trauma is ongoing. This dorsal vagal complex facilitates an immobilization response in order to conserve energy which, in turn, helps you survive. When in this state, you might feel shut down, numb, foggy, fatigued, low energy, and in some cases, dizzy or nauseous. It is common to feel this way for days or even months, and these symptoms can persist even though the traumatic events are over. Furthermore, minor stressors can reactivate this nervous system state, making recovery challenging.

In contrast, the myelinated ventral vagal complex allows you to rest in stillness for the purpose of bonding and connection. Dr. Porges refers to this branch of the vagus nerve as the "social engagement system," because we are biologically wired to connect to each other. Doing so has ensured the survival of our species. We have gathered together as tribes for eons to share resources and protect each other from predators. Together, we have engaged in rituals of dance, music, and storytelling in order to not only survive, but also thrive. Not only does the ventral vagal circuit promote social connection, it also helps you respond to cues of safety in the voice tone, facial expressions, and caring presence of others. While the social engagement system benefits from the regulating presence of others, you can also tap into the healing power of your vagus nerve by exploring practices that help you access that warm feeling of safety and connection within yourself. These practices can be done on your own, anywhere and anytime, to enhance your physical, emotional, and mental health.

The practices you will learn in this workbook will focus on increasing your *vagal tone*. Simply put, optimal vagal tone allows the two primary branches of your autonomic nervous system to work in a balanced manner. This harmonious equilibrium reduces your experience of anxiety, stress, or depression—and perhaps most importantly, increases or enhances your physical health, improves your mental clarity, and supports a general sense of well-being (McCraty and Childre 2010). You are able to rest into the nourishing benefits of the parasympathetic system, which helps you rest, relax, sleep well, and connect meaningfully with yourself and others. In addition, you will feel more energized during the day, so that you can engage in your life in a more fulfilling manner.

Roadmap to Resilience

You are not only biologically wired to respond to threats; you are also endowed with an intrinsic capacity to recover from traumatic stress. Polyvagal theory provides you with a roadmap to resilience, allowing you to reclaim your health and vitality. The tools offered in this book do not erase the traumatic events that happened to you. However, you can recover from the symptoms of post-traumatic stress. Resilience helps you feel capable of working through the pain of the past while feeling empowered in the present and hopeful about your future. Rather than isolating yourself or withdrawing from life, you can tap into resilience to engage wholeheartedly with the world, while trusting in your capacity to respond to difficulty when it arises.

Resilience is sometimes misunderstood as solely an internal process. Sadly, when we do not feel resilient, we are apt to blame ourselves. However, resilience requires that we have access to relational support systems such as therapy, a good friend, or a family member who cares about you, and safe community spaces. Likewise, polyvagal theory recognizes that we need to feel valued and experience a sense of belonging in order to heal. Once we feel supported and connected to these external resources, we are generally more able to access an internal wellspring of compassion and wisdom. You can build resilience by working through difficult experiences and feelings, while recognizing that doing so can help you learn more about yourself. Even though you might want to give up or withdraw from the world, it is your commitment to the ongoing process of trauma recovery that ultimately helps you grow stronger as a person.

Navigating Barriers to Trauma Recovery

One of the biggest challenges when reading any workbook for self-care is that we often avoid engaging in the very things that would help us heal. If you find it difficult to make the time for yourself, you are not alone. This too is one of the symptoms of post-traumatic stress. Take some time to review these common barriers to self-care and explore these suggestions to help you navigate a path forward.

1. **You resist self-care:** Like many of us, you may have internalized messages that making time for yourself is selfish or greedy. As a result, you might feel ashamed of your needs or unworthy of taking time for yourself. To navigate this barrier, it is important to build a new narrative about your self-worth. Taking time for yourself is necessary for your well-being. Self-care is not selfish—it is essential.

2. **You fear becoming overwhelmed:** You might feel frightened that if you slow down or take the time to connect to your body, you will feel overwhelmed by your emotions. While it is true that our bodies carry our wounds, healing does not require that you consistently confront your pain. Instead, healing invites you to recognize that you can be in charge of where you focus your attention. In addition to attending to the wounds of trauma, you also learn to build positive resources by cultivating experiences in which you feel safe, at ease, relaxed, and peaceful. You can adjust the pace of your healing process. Practice placing disturbing feelings into a container where they can be held temporarily while you attend to other aspect of your life, such as raising kids, going to work, or sleeping well at night. When creating a container, you can visualize a box, file cabinet, or room big enough to hold the disturbing feelings or images. Then, return your attention to your current environment and any cues that let you know that you are safe enough now. You can unpack the container and attend to your pain at the right time, when you have the right amount of support, such as in therapy.

3. **You feel isolated in your healing journey:** With a history of trauma, you might feel burdened by beliefs that you do not belong or that you are unlovable. These beliefs can lead you to further isolate yourself from others. We all need to feel connected to others. Positive and caring social connections help us heal. To navigate this barrier, you might seek out meet-up organizations or therapeutic groups focused on healing and creating safe spaces for connection. If you have difficulty finding these spaces in your local community, many are available through the internet, which offers a safe and accessible way to meet other people.

4. **You have a pervasive feeling of powerlessness:** Have you experienced times in your life where no matter what you did, you couldn't change your circumstances? Maybe you couldn't stop your parents from drinking, hurting each other, or hurting you. Or perhaps you have been discriminated against and unprotected by your

community or country. In these cases, it is common to feel voiceless and powerless. As a result, you might believe that no matter how hard you work, your efforts will never make a difference in the outcome of your day, week, or life. While there will always be experiences that are out of your control, attending to your nervous system will positively influence how you treat yourself and navigate the world around you. Even if some days are difficult, your willingness to engage in positive actions— even small ones—will begin to make a difference in your life.

Perhaps you can relate to these common barriers to trauma recovery. What messages, thoughts, or beliefs keep you from engaging in a healing journey?

_____

_____

_____

_____

_____

_____

_____

_____

_____

_____

Write down any new messages would you like to tell yourself now that give you a sense of hope for the future.

_____

_____

_____

_____

_____

_____

_____

_____

_____

_____

_____

_____

_____

How to Get the Most out of This Workbook

Before we move forward, I'll offer a few more tips to help you get the most out of this workbook, as you navigate the healing path ahead.

- **Identify your ideal practice time and space:** Consistency can be valuable when beginning any new practice. What time of day is best for you? Do you prefer morning or evening? Where would you like to be when you explore these practices? Be realistic about the challenges that might interfere with your ability to engage with these practices. For example, if you tend to be distracted by your phone, can you put it in another room during your practice time? Or, if you are a parent, can you ask someone to watch your children while you engage in self-care?

- **Start small:** It can feel overwhelming to start anything new. When you're standing at the bottom of the mountain, the climb might feel insurmountable. In these moments, it can be beneficial to focus on the small steps, or on one small change you can make today. I suggest setting aside fifteen to twenty minutes a day to engage with this workbook; however, if five minutes is where you need to begin, honor your process. Whenever you do engage in a practice, take the time to appreciate yourself for your efforts.

- **Follow your intuition:** You might initially read through this workbook from beginning to end; however, once you become familiar with the exercises, allow yourself to progress intuitively. Some of the practices might feel more accessible than others. It is okay to skip any practices if they feel uncomfortable. The goal of this book is to strengthen your access to resources; you will build your capacity to handle increasing amounts of challenge over time.

- **Partner with a friend or family member:** Find an accountability partner who is willing to explore each exercise with you. This is especially valuable since polyvagal theory recognizes the importance of social connections as a foundation for healing. Set up a plan to text or talk to each other on a regular basis, such as once a day or once a week. If possible, engage in the practices together.

- **Use the journaling prompts to track your progress:** Sometimes growth is slow and imperceptible in the moment. However, over time, these small changes can accumulate. When you write about your experiences, you can go back and reflect on how you have changed throughout the course of using this workbook.

- **Work with a psychotherapist:** This healing professional will help hold space for any vulnerable feelings that arise along the way. If possible, look for someone who is trauma-informed, body-centered, and trained in polyvagal theory. However, the most important component of successful therapy is that you feel safe, understood, and compassionately accepted for who you are.

What would you like to get out of this workbook? What are your biggest hopes? Write down some goals.

_____

_____

_____

_____

_____

_____

_____

_____

_____

_____

Do you have any worries or fears about moving forward? Write them down.

_____

_____

_____

_____

_____

_____

_____

_____

Who might accompany you on your journey? What current support systems do you have? What additional supports do you need? Name the people and resources you can rely on as you go through this workbook.

_____

_____

_____

_____

_____

Looking Ahead

Throughout these pages, you will have opportunities to build an inner sanctuary of resources in support of your journey through trauma recovery. You will get to know your nervous system through practices that help rewire your resilience. Each chapter offers opportunities for self-reflection, with journaling prompts to help you get the most out of this workbook. As you begin, I invite you to take a moment to pause and reflect on how trauma has impacted your life. While doing so can be difficult, this can help you feel motivated to engage in your healing journey.

What repercussions have traumatic events had on you physically, emotionally, or mentally?

_____

_____

_____

_____

_____

_____

How have these events impacted your relationships?

_____

_____

_____

_____

_____

_____

What have you already explored to help you attend to the weight of traumatic events? What has worked for you thus far?

_____

_____

_____

_____

_____

_____

Where have you felt stuck along the way?

_____

_____

_____

_____

_____

_____

Can you sense a new set of possibilities by focusing on the applied science of safety? Write about how your life might change if you felt safe.

_____

_____

_____

_____

_____

_____

_____

_____

_____

_____

_____

_____

_____

_____

Applied polyvagal theory is a gentle and kind approach to healing that serves as a foundation for trauma recovery. I hope that you find this to be the case for you. Remember, you are not alone in your journey. I am here to serve as your guide.

Polyvagal Theory Is the Science of Safety

It is easy to feel overwhelmed by the events of our world. Thanks to the news, we are confronted with tragedies and losses on a daily basis. Too often, our nervous systems are inundated by the endless waves of information that come toward us at lightning speed through social media. While you might swipe away from disturbing images or stories, they have often already left an imprint that can amplify your anxiety or a general feeling of threat. When you have a history of personal trauma, the responses that we all have to world events can be amplified. You can more easily feel thrown out of balance, and it may be more difficult for you to recover. Simply put, you feel less resilient.

This chapter explores polyvagal theory—the science of safety—in depth. We will look at the symptoms of post-traumatic stress disorder (PTSD) and dissociation through the lens of the nervous system. Keep in mind that your nervous system is wired for survival, and your body helps you respond to threats within a fraction of a second. Therefore, healing requires slowing down and paying attention to the cues that let you know that you are safe here and now. You will learn key tools for building a felt sense of ease and connection with yourself, others, and the world around you. You will discover why body awareness helps you move away from narratives that can exacerbate the symptoms of trauma. In time and with practice, you can develop your capacity to feel more resourced, and as a result, less distressed by the traumatic events of your past, so that you can live fully and rest easily.

Evolution, Survival, and Your Threat Response

Polyvagal theory represents an evolutionary series of defenses that has helped both animals and humans survive. Millions of years ago, the earliest animal species had primitive nervous systems. When confronted with a threat, these early animals sometimes survived by withdrawing or hiding to avoid being sensed by a predator. They camouflaged themselves with their surroundings, immobilized into complete stillness, or slowed down their breathing and heart rate to avoid being detected. From the perspective of polyvagal theory, this defense strategy relies on the dorsal vagal complex.

As animals evolved, so did their range of self-protective behaviors. They relied more heavily on their ability to flee from danger or attack predators. These behaviors use the sympathetic nervous system. Looking more closely at the evolution of mammals, we can also see a more advanced strategy for survival, which enhances our ability to be connected to each other: Imagine a pack of wolves, a herd of elephants, or a group of chimpanzees. They gather in groups to fend off predators, find warmth, access food, and seek comfort. From the perspective of polyvagal theory, this capacity to bond with others requires that we let go of the more primitive defense strategies of feigning death, fight, or flight (Porges 2011). Instead, we rely on the more recently evolved ventral vagal complex—our social engagement system. This allows us to nurse babies and bond with our children.

Polyvagal theory recognizes that we as humans evolved the same survival strategies seen in animals. When we feel safe, we are more likely to seek connection with each other through the ventral vagal circuit. We are able to feel compassion, comfort others, and behave generously. We are also more likely to feel lovingly connected to ourselves. However, when we are in danger, we progress through a predictable set of responses that reverse the evolutionary trajectory just described. This is referred to as the *tiered response to threat*. Initially, we might attempt to resolve a threat by reestablishing social connection. We call out to others or reach out our hands for help. If we are unable to restore a sense of safety and connection, we devolve into relying on our sympathetic nervous system in order to flee or fight off the danger. If this is unsuccessful, we regress into the dorsal vagal circuit, which immobilizes us into what's called a feigned death response. In this state, we might literally faint, want to withdraw or hide, or feel helpless, powerless, dizzy, nauseous, fatigued, or collapsed.

Polyvagal theory provides a compassionate way of understanding your own threat responses by recognizing that your nervous system is working hard to ensure your survival. If you relate to the tiered response to threat, you are not alone. Take some time to reflect on this for yourself with the following questions. If you would like, use the spaces below to create a picture of what each nervous system state feels like for you. You might choose a color that represents each state or create an image that shows how you feel in each state.

Ventral vagal: Can you think of times when you have felt safe, connected, nurtured, peaceful, or at ease? Create an image that represents feeling safe and connected.

Sympathetic: Can you think of times when you have wanted to run away or protect yourself from a frightening situation? Create an image that represents being in your fight-or-flight system.

Dorsal vagal: Can you recall times in which you felt small, voiceless, powerless, or shut down? Create an image that represents feeling shut down or withdrawn.

As you progress through these pages, you will learn the tools to come out of survival and reclaim your birthright of connection to yourself, others, and the world around you.

How PTSD Affects Sensory Processing

Your body's threat responses are involuntary. They are your nervous system's ways of signaling that you do not feel safe. Your sensory processing systems help you navigate these threats. Moreover, they do so automatically. This is a good thing. You do not want to have to stop and think if you have touched a hot stove—and luckily, you don't have to think. These quick, reflexive responses are necessary for your survival.

Your body has multiple sensory processing systems. The first of these is *exteroception*—the five senses that let you see, hear, smell, touch, and taste. When you have experienced a traumatic event, it is common for this sensory system to feel heightened. You might feel sensitive to loud noises or startle easily. Or, certain smells might lead you to recall disturbing memories. The second sensory processing system is *interoception*—the processing of internal bodily sensations, such as changes in temperature, hunger, thirst, sleepiness, alertness, tension, and pain. Paying attention to your body lets you observe when you are feeling an emotion. For example, you might notice a heaviness in your chest or a knot in your throat. Once again, trauma can interfere with your interoceptive awareness, leading you to feel hyperaware of discomfort or dissociated from your sensations. Your third sensory system is *proprioception*, which lets you feel where your body is in space, helping with coordination and balance. A history of trauma can lead you to feel clumsy or awkward in your movements. All of these systems are working together to provide you with feedback that forms the foundation of your sense of self in the world. However, as you can see, trauma can alter your sensory processing and can profoundly impact how you perceive yourself and the world around you (Harricharan, McKinnon, and Lanius 2021).

Within polyvagal theory, there is a fourth sensory processing system called *neuroception*, which refers to the way your nervous system is wired to detect whether situations or people are safe, dangerous, or life threatening (Porges 2004). As with the other sensory processing systems, neuroception occurs without conscious awareness. For example, when you walk into a room full of people, your nervous system begins to scan your environment. Without even realizing why, you might begin to feel on guard, anxious, or agitated. This is because your nervous system is scanning for cues of threat, and once one is identified, your system proceeds to send signals throughout your brain and body to release stress chemicals such as cortisol and adrenaline. This increases your heart rate, leads you to breathe faster, and engages your muscles in preparation for fight or flight. All of this can occur within a fraction of a second.

When you are in danger, responding defensively is necessary for your survival. Unfortunately, sometimes the threat is over, but you are still reacting to relatively harmless sensory experiences as if you are in danger. For example, you might startle or scream if a door closes loudly or a person unexpectedly comes up behind you. In that case, like a false alarm, your nervous system is responding as if you are in danger even when there is no current threat. This kind of mismatch between your nervous system and your environment occurs as a result of an overactive sympathetic nervous system. In this case, you are more likely to feel hypervigilant and highly alert to your surroundings. You are likely to feel jumpy and restless, or perhaps prone to irritability and anger. This forms the basis of PTSD.

The Symptoms of PTSD

Eric served in the military and experienced traumatic events that continued to haunt him years later. He wanted to be present with his wife and daughter, but struggled to cope with memories and nightmares that haunted him. He described feeling on edge and quick to anger. Simple tasks like going to the grocery store or attending social gatherings became overwhelming for him. Sometimes his hypervigilance or irritability would lead him to react strongly in front of his family, which evoked feelings of shame. He began avoiding other people because he simply couldn't handle being triggered and feeling out of control.

Eric's story is common and reveals the most commonly identified symptoms of PTSD, which typically fall into three categories: reexperiencing, avoidance, and heightened arousal.

- Reexperiencing might involve having intrusive memories from the past or flashbacks that evoke disturbing emotions or sensations. You might have nightmares that interfere with your ability to sleep at night.

- Avoidance symptoms might lead you to stay away from people or places that are reminders of the traumatic event. You might isolate yourself. Another form of avoidance is pushing away your feelings through the use of food, alcohol, drugs, extreme exercise, staying busy, or working excessively.

- Heightened arousal can lead you to feel hypervigilant of your surroundings. You might feel on guard and tense, or you might startle easily in response to noises and unexpected movement.

PTSD was initially thought to only manifest as these high-arousal symptoms; however, there is another form of post-traumatic stress that develops in response to ongoing, repeated, and chronic traumatization that often begins in childhood. This is complex post-traumatic stress disorder (CPTSD), and it is characterized by low-arousal symptoms such as fatigue, disorientation, and dissociation. Let's take a look at Alexis's experience:

Alexis grew up in a home with parents who were self-absorbed and unavailable. Her father was often out of the house working. Her mother was overwhelmed with the three children. She was bullied and physically abused by her older brother; however, when she cried or called out to her parents, she was blamed and told she was the problem. Alexis struggled with sensing her body and feeling her emotions. She described living in a fog and had a difficult time realizing that what she went through wasn't okay. She continued to carry shame about her past and deeply believed that there was something wrong with her. As a result, she struggled to feel worthy in relationships and would often settle for partners who treated her poorly.

As you can see in Alexis's case, CPTSD symptoms might lead to the following categories of symptoms: emotional distress, negative self-concept, and interpersonal difficulties.

- Emotional distress can show up in a variety of ways, such as periods of anxiety, irritability, or anger followed by feelings of hopelessness and despair. Sometimes, you might feel numb and disconnected from your emotions all together. If you were exposed to ongoing trauma in your childhood or left feeling unsafe in the world, you might have had to become very sensitive to your environment and other people's behaviors. Your sensitivity to the voice tone, body language, and facial expressions of others may have been necessary to navigate the world. Feeling highly sensitized to other people's moods or threats might be emotionally dysregulating.

- Having a negative self-concept is a result of internalizing inaccurate and damaging beliefs about yourself, which can lead you to carry excessive guilt, shame, and self-blame about the events of your life. You might inaccurately believe that you are at fault, damaged, or worthless.

- Interpersonal difficulties often arise when you have a history of relational trauma. You might not know how to trust others or you might feel deeply afraid of being abandoned by others. In some cases, you might enter into hurtful relationships because they feel familiar to you or because you do not believe you deserve to be treated with kindness and respect.

In contrast to the overactive sympathetic nervous system that is seen in the classic presentation of PTSD, CPTSD often engages the dorsal vagal circuit, meaning that the parasympathetic nervous system is responding to threat. In this case, you might be more likely to be underreactive to your environment. You might not engage your defensive, self-protective response in a situation that is actually unsafe. It is as if there is a fire in the house, but no alarms are signaling the danger. This underreactive nervous system typically occurs when there is a life-threatening event or chronic trauma from which there is no way to escape. For example, if you grew up in an unsafe environment, you may have coped by dissociating from the sensory reality of the danger that surrounded you. Any child raised by parents or caregivers who were repeatedly unsafe would naturally want to protect themselves from the threat. However, if they were unable to protect themselves or physically run away, then the only option would be to mentally "run away" by retreating and withdrawing into the recesses of their own mind. Dissociation engages a dorsal vagal response and allows you to disconnect from the felt experience of danger in order to survive.

As children, we are dependent on our parents and caregivers; we need to attach to them in order to survive. When parents are neglectful, abusive, or using substances, it is often necessary for the child to make the parents "safe enough," so that the child can uphold the relationship. This can result the child having in a fantasy about "the good parent" as a way to protect themselves from the reality of the frightful and dangerous parent. If this is true for you, you may have dissociated from your instinctual knowing that the parent's voice tone, facial expressions, body language, or behavior was threatening. The tendency to dissociate from your sensory reality might lead you to engage in risky behaviors without sensing the danger. For example, you might enter into unsafe relationships while ignoring the red flags of the other person's threatening body language or voice tone.

In order to come out of a dorsal vagal response and dissociation, it is necessary to return to your senses. This process involves gently and slowly returning your awareness to your body. Honoring your pace with this process is key to success, and the tools you will learn throughout this workbook will guide you one step at a time.

For the first step, look over the symptoms and descriptions of PTSD and CPTSD. How do they show up for you? Notice if there is any shame or self-judgment arising as you write about your symptoms. As much as possible, I encourage you to be gentle with yourself.

_____

_____

_____

_____

_____

_____

_____

_____

_____

_____

_____

_____

_____

Whether you are overreactive or underreactive to your environment, I encourage you to recognize that your nervous system has been trying to protect you. Once again, polyvagal theory invites you to reflect on your past with compassion.

Cultivate Nervous System Awareness

While neuroception leads you to respond to potential sources of threat automatically, you can also learn to consciously assess whether your nervous system response is necessary. Moreover, if you determine that you are actually safe here and now, you can learn to come out of any unnecessary stress responses. You do so by bringing conscious perception to the cues that let you know what nervous system state you are currently in.

Cultivating nervous system awareness requires that you pay attention to your bodily felt sense. This process allows you to determine whether you feel safe, on guard, or shut down. If you are feeling unsafe, you are more likely to have a dry mouth, sweaty palms, a fast heartbeat stomach pain, or nausea; be short of breath; or feel restless or tense in your arms, legs, chest, or jaw. Paying attention to your body also helps you sense when you are safe. In times of safety, you are more likely to breathe effortlessly, be capable of resting in stillness, and feel a warmth in your chest, a steadiness to your heartbeat, be relaxed in your muscles, and settled in your stomach.

Sensing your body might feel challenging for you. You might be worried about becoming overwhelmed, or you might feel numb and disconnected from your body. In either case, what matters is progressing with self-awareness of your sensations at a pace that you can tolerate. Take a moment to reflect on how your body provides you with feedback about your nervous system state. Take a look at the following chart of body symptoms that indicate sympathetic activation, dorsal vagal threat response, and ventral vagal relaxation response.

EXERCISE
Check In with Your Body Symptoms

Circle or highlight how you are feeling now.

Ventral Vagal: Relaxation Response	Sympathetic: Stress Activation	Dorsal Vagal: Threat Response
I feel connected to my body.	I feel acutely aware of my body.	I feel disconnected from my body.
My breathing feels relaxed.	My breathing is rapid.	It takes effort to breathe.
I can breathe fully.	I feel short of breath.	My breathing is shallow.
I can think clearly.	My thoughts are racing.	My head feels foggy.
My voice tone feels soothing.	My voice is strained.	My voice is flat and lacks energy.
I can communicate easily.	I am speaking rapidly.	It is hard for me to talk.
My face feels relaxed.	My jaw is tense.	My face feels tired.
My eyes are soft.	My brow is furrowed.	My eyes look dull.
I feel calm and at ease.	I feel agitated and irritable.	I feel withdrawn and shut down.
It is easy to rest in stillness.	I am restless and jumpy.	I feel lethargic.
I feel present.	I feel overwhelmed.	I feel far away.

Most of us will experience different nervous system states at different times, with different people, and in different settings. You can practice enhancing awareness of your nervous system state at any time by downloading this chart from http://www.newharbinger.com/54162 and referring to it whenever you want to check in with yourself.

Gently Pay Attention to Your Body's Felt Sense

You do not need to rush the healing process. If you notice that you are feeling unnecessarily keyed up in anxiety or shut down and withdrawn, you can counterbalance these defensive states by focusing on cues in your environment that help you know that you are safe enough. This will allow your body and mind to relax and heal. Use your five senses. Notice what you see and hear. Notice any smells in your environment. Your sensory awareness will also allow you to assess whether you are accurately responding to your current circumstances. If you are currently unsafe, you can take action to restore safety by seeking protection or leaving an unsafe environment.

If there are no current threats, it is likely your internal sensations are related to memories of threat from the past. If this is true for you, pay attention to external cues of safety, and see if you can help your body and brain understand that you are safe now. Is there anything that you can look at, touch, listen to, taste, or smell that will help you feel more peaceful and at ease? For example, it can be helpful to put on your favorite music, enjoy the scent of your favorite essential oil, or put your feet on the earth and sense the ground beneath you. Adding in sensory resources that help you feel safe here and now can help you reduce feelings of overwhelm. Try it now.

EXERCISE
Sensing Safety

Step 1: Tune into your body's felt sense and record what you notice here.

_____

_____

_____

Step 2: Do you feel safe in this moment?   Circle: **Yes**   **No**

Step 3: If you do not feel safe, observe your environment. Write down what you notice.

_____

_____

_____

Step 4: Now that you have observed your environment, can you identify if you are safe enough right here and now?

Circle: **Yes   No**

Step 5: If you are unsafe, what can you do to seek protection or leave the situation? If you are safe in your current circumstances, write down some resources you can see, touch, taste, smell, or hear that are soothing and help you feel peaceful.

_____

_____

_____

_____

The Negativity Bias

With a history of trauma, you might be prone to ruminating about the past or worrying about the future. You might notice your body and mind feel vigilantly reactive to the world, which can disrupt your ability to sleep at night or relax fully. Imagining worst-case scenarios can lead you to worry about leaving the house, visiting with friends, or opening up to the world. These tendencies can lead you to isolate from others or disengage from living your best life.

Your nervous system is wired to help you survive, using the past to help you predict the future. In other words, you might have a tendency to review memories of times you felt threatened, hurt, or betrayed, because this helps you anticipate or prevent bad things from happening in the future. Unfortunately, when you have a history of trauma, these disturbing memories outweigh and override your ability to recall times of ease or notice that you are safe now. This is referred to as the *negativity bias*, and it is biologically wired into your nervous system (Hanson 2016).

Continually focusing on potential threats can impede your growth. In order to heal, you can gently invite your mind to let go of the tendency to ruminate about the past or worry about the future by focusing on present. Of course, this is easier said than done. Letting go can feel scary. Maybe you feel like you will not be able to protect yourself if you soften your vigilance. Or perhaps feelings of grief arise in the process. This is all normal and why self-compassion is a key element of the healing journey. Focusing on cues of ease, beauty, or safety might not come naturally at first—it is a skill that requires practice. For example, you might say, "I see the vase of flowers, I notice the sunlight pouring through the window, I like the painting on my wall." This process allows your body and mind to move out of stressful states. Try it now:

Turn your head from side to side and write down what you can see, hear, or touch that provides you with cues that you are safe now. Find one thing in your current environment that inspires a feeling of calm or ease.

_____

_____

_____

_____

_____

Bring to mind times and places when you felt safe, peaceful, at ease, or relaxed. For example, you might recall a vacation you took to the beach or a recent visit with a caring friend. What people, pets, or places have historically brought you a sense of ease? What do you notice now as you remember these sources of safety?

_____

_____

_____

_____

_____

_____

EXERCISE
Overcoming Negativity Bias

You can counterbalance negativity bias by cultivating simple moments of peace. Perhaps this involves reading a favorite book, listening to a soothing song, or watching a movie that makes you laugh. Once you have accessed a feeling of joy, savor that positive state by pausing for at least thirty seconds. Allow your body and mind to fully absorb the experience. Make a list of things that bring you peace, beauty, or joy.

1. _____

2. _____

3. _____

4. _____

5. _____

6. _____

7. _____

8. _____

9. _____

10. _____

Focusing on positive life moments does not negate the challenges of stressful or traumatic life events. However, it does allow you to build a broader capacity to feel safe enough in the present moment. This strengthens your ability to compassionately attend to the pain from your past or your fears of your future. In other words, in order to heal, you must recognize that you are so much more than your pain.

Polyvagal Theory and Trauma Recovery

Polyvagal theory provides you with a map to find freedom from the defensive states of your nervous system. When you feel safe in the present moment, you can develop a refined and renewed relationship with both your sympathetic and your parasympathetic nervous system states. The ventral vagal complex on its own is associated with feeling calm, connected, and compassionate with yourself and others. You can also combine your ventral vagal circuit with your sympathetic nervous system, which is known as a hybrid nervous system state (Porges 2017). Now, instead of moving into a fight-or-flight response, your sympathetic nervous system allows you to move your body in the context of safety. This gives you the energy to play, go to a dance class, climb a mountain, or lift weights at the gym. You are more likely to feel empowered and motivated to meet your goals. Explore for yourself whether there are places, people, or activities that help you safely and playfully access your sympathetic system. For example, you might enjoy hiking in the mountains, attending a dance class, going to an amusement park, or being around friends who lovingly encourage you to challenge yourself.

Identify times when you were able to move your body in an energetic, playful, or creative way that left you feeling joyful and excited. Write down the places, people, and activities that help you access this empowered state of your hybrid nervous system.

_____

_____

_____

_____

_____

_____

_____

You can also blend the ventral vagal complex with the dorsal vagal complex. This hybrid state allows you to access the relaxation response, which allows you to rest and digest (Benson and Proctor 2011). This state gives you the ability to rest into stillness without feeling collapsed, which improves sleep and allows your body to heal from illness. This state will also help you access the nourishment of feeling compassionately connected with others. Once again, you might notice specific places, people, or activities that evoke this nervous system state. For example, you might recall relaxing at the beach on a sunny day, sitting in a guided relaxation practice, or receiving a hug from a person who feels safe and caring.

Identify times when you have been able to rest and relax without feeling collapsed or shut down. What places, people, or activities help you access this restorative state of your nervous system? Write them down.

_____

_____

_____

_____

_____

_____

_____

_____

_____

_____

Parasympathetic ventral vagal (social engagement system):

Safe enough, calm, connected

Sympathetic with ventral safety:

Play, excitement, exercise, empowerment

Parasympathetic dorsal vagal with ventral safety:

Rest and digest

Sympathetic threat response:

Fight, flight

Parasympathetic dorsal vagal threat response:

Withdrawal, collapse, fatigue, feigned death

When applying polyvagal theory to healing, the first step is to recognize the state of your nervous system, which is accomplished by paying attention to your body. This allows you to notice whether you are feeling safe and at ease, keyed up in your sympathetic nervous system, or shut down in the dorsal vagal complex. Self-knowledge is a key to successful change. You can counterbalance any tendencies to focus on your fears by paying attention to and savoring moments of safety, beauty, and connection. Cultivating these positive states on a regular basis nourishes your nervous system.

CHAPTER 2

The Gift of Connection

Polyvagal theory recognizes that your nervous system is wired for and strengthened by connection, whether that is with yourself, others, or even a beloved pet (Cozolino 2014). The myelinated ventral vagus nerve, or "social engagement system," has neural connections into your eyes, the muscles of your face, your inner ear, and the vocalization muscles in your throat. This allows you to communicate how you feel to others through your facial expressions and voice tone. You also receive other people's expressions and tone through your eyes and ears. It is through these connections with others that we tend to find a sense of solace, safety, and inner calm. You can imagine a mother offering her calm presence to a child through her loving gaze, soft voice, and soothing lullaby. Or a caring friend offering compassion through a kind smile. Perhaps you can recall a time of genuine connection and notice how your body responds as you reflect on that experience. You might even sense how you naturally take a sigh and soften in the loving presence of another.

We all need these caring connections with others in order to heal from trauma. However, many traumatic events take a toll on our relationships with others. You may have been harmed by another person, whether as a result of untrustworthy or incompetent caregivers during childhood, unsafe relationships in your adult life, or a lack of protection in community spaces. As a result, you might have had few soothing and caring connections with others. You might not trust others, or you might push well-intended people away. Perhaps you fear being abandoned, or maybe you lose touch with yourself and your own needs when you are in relationships with others. If so, you are not alone; these are common experiences when you have lived through relational trauma.

Polyvagal theory provides a pathway of repair and hope, along with guidance about how to navigate these wounds. You can develop your ability to find healthy, meaningful connections with others while staying true to yourself. In part, this process involves seeking out the presence of caring people in your life now. This lets you experience the benefits of positive, trustworthy, and nurturing relationships. Initially, the safest place to find this reparative connection might be in psychotherapy, with a trained professional who is capable of helping you navigate the relational wounds of your past.

Having a sense of belonging is essential for our well-being. Unfortunately, traumatic events can interfere with this sense of belonging, especially if you felt betrayed by your family, community, or country. Therefore, having group therapeutic spaces can also be an essential part of your healing journey. Group spaces provide opportunities for you to experience and receive the gift of being welcomed by others who are in their own process of trauma recovery. As you trust in your own capacity to skillfully navigate interpersonal connections, you can bring the skills you are learning in this book with you into your personal relationships as well, such as with a family member, caring friend, or intimate partner.

Having meaningful connections with others is only part of the picture. Healthy relationships with others also require that you cultivate a compassionate relationship to yourself. You create this compassionate relationship every time you hold yourself with tenderness, kindness, and self-acceptance. This ground of safety within yourself helps you create nourishing experiences with others, such as offering your undivided attention to a friend.

This chapter explores how we are wired by and for connection. We will discuss the impact of attachment in childhood development and how these early experiences influence the development of your vagus nerve. There are healing practices, journaling prompts to enhance self-awareness, and guided practices to cultivate self-compassion. Ultimately, the gift of connection can ripple outward and shape how you show up in larger spheres of your life—at work, in your community, or as a beneficial presence in the world.

Before we move on, take a moment to reflect on a person from your past or present who has been a source of kindness, nurturing, and compassion for you. If you cannot recall a person from your life, you can also build this resource using a public figure, such as TV program host Mr. Rogers as a source of wisdom and compassion, or a fictional character, animal, or spiritual being, such as a guardian angel as loving support. You could even imagine what your beloved pet would say to you if they could speak. These people, spiritual resources, or animals will serve as allies who support and protect you as you heal from trauma.

Reflect on time(s) in your life when you felt valued and respected. Who has helped you feel accepted, understood, heard, and cared for? Write their names on the lines below.

Bring to mind a historical or public figure, spiritual being, or animal who represents the qualities of nurturance and care. These characters can be real, fictional, or imagined. Write their names on the lines below.

_____

_____

_____

_____

_____

Imagine your team of relational allies (real or imagined) together with you, supporting you. They are here to compassionately accept you as you are. Write down how you feel as you visualize this team around you.

_____

_____

_____

_____

_____

_____

_____

_____

I invite you to bring your relational allies to mind anytime you feel vulnerable. If you found this exercise challenging, a trustworthy psychotherapist is trained to provide these nurturing experiences in relationship.

Let's Start at the Very Beginning

Our experience of relationships in the world starts with our earliest life experiences. From the perspective of the polyvagal theory, the ABCs of relational health can be thought of as *Attachment*, *Bonding*, and *Coregulation*. Let's take a closer look.

The vagus nerve begins to develop during the third trimester of pregnancy. Stressful or traumatic events during a mother's pregnancy, such as domestic violence or the death of a loved one, can negatively impact the health of the mother's vagus nerve. Likewise, when a mother has depression, anxiety, unresolved PTSD, or uses substances, her vagus nerve can be negatively impacted as measured by reduced *vagal ton*e. Vagal tone is a measure of the nervous system's capacity to handle stress. Lower vagal tone is associated with a decreased capacity to effectively respond to and recover from everyday challenges.

When a mother has lower vagal tone during pregnancy, her infant is more likely to have a lower birth weight, be prone to colic, and be difficult to soothe (Thomson 2007). When a mother has a reduced capacity to handle stress and her baby is more difficult to soothe, we often see a vicious cycle of emotional dysregulation, in which both the parent and the child remain in states of distress for extended periods (Rattaz et al. 2022; Wesarg et al. 2022).

Even with an optimal prenatal experience, an infant's vagus nerve is not fully developed at birth. Infants require the presence of their caregivers to help them regulate their immature nervous systems. Vagal tone is strengthened through a *secure attachment relationship.*

Attachment is a source of connection that occurs between two people. Initially, this is experienced between an infant and a caregiver. Secure attachment is built when you have a reliable and trustworthy caregiver who provides care in a consistent and predictable manner.

Bonding refers to the connection that is built between a caregiver and infant. Bonds of connection and safety are cultivated through a synchronized dance of touch, vocalizations, facial expressions, and body language. Simply put, all of these nonverbal exchanges help the infant feel safe.

Coregulation refers to the calming and soothing presence that one person offers another. This happens when one person is well-established within their ventral vagal—social engagement—system and can provide that system's calming influence to another. This might look like holding, rocking, or singing a lullaby to a child who is afraid or sad. In time, that consistent loving presence forms the basis of a secure sense of self for the child.

While parenting doesn't have to be perfect, when a child does not have enough of the ABCs, they are more likely to develop an *attachment wound*. Attachment wounds are described in three categories, each of which develops with the interactional style of a caregiver:

- **Insecure-avoidant attachment:** This attachment style develops when a child had a distant or disengaged caregiver, and adapted by avoiding closeness, disconnecting from their own emotions, or becoming overly self-reliant. As adults, they tend to be dismissive of their own and other people's emotions, and they have difficulty accepting their own and others' needs for connection.

- **Anxious-ambivalent attachment:** This attachment style develops when a child had an inconsistent caregiver who was at times highly responsive and perceptive, but could also be intrusive and invasive. The child tends to feel plagued by uncertainty and feelings of anxiety. As adults, they are easily emotionally overwhelmed and may fear abandonment and being rejected. They are often driven by a need to seek closeness and may come across as overly dependent on others.

- **Disorganized attachment:** This attachment style develops when a child has grown up with a caregiver whose behavior was alarming or threatening. They often feel caught inside of a double bind—trapped between their biological drive to seek closeness with a parent and their biological drive to flee when that parent is a source of danger. As adults, they struggle in relationships with others and may rely on impulsive or aggressive behaviors when their own need for attachment and connection arises.

Keep in mind that most of us do not develop a single attachment style; rather, we cultivate strategies to maintain the sense of connection that we so deeply need in order to survive (Cowan and Cowan 2007). In addition, we tend to develop different attachment strategies within different relationships in childhood. Let's look at an example:

Sara grew up with her mother, grandparents, and aunt. Sara's father left her and her mother before her first birthday, and Sara and her mother moved in with her grandparents. Sara's mother was often fighting with her parents. Sara often felt frightened by her mother, who would come and go erratically, leaving her feeling anxious. Deep inside, she also felt rejection and abandonment from the father she never knew. She wondered why he left her behind.

Sometimes, she felt overwhelmed by all that she experienced growing up, which led to feelings of anger and irritability. In that disorganized state, she struggled to know what to do with all of the feelings that would build up inside of her. When asked if she recalled any moments of comfort or security growing up, Sara described her aunt as a source of calm. She was a source of kindness and reliability in a home that was largely unpredictable. As a result, Sara carried within her a deep sense of what it meant to feel safe and connected. This became a source of inner calm that helped Sara develop a secure sense of herself.

Within Sara's story, we hear of different sources of attachment within her family of origin. Think of attachment as a pie with different-size slices that represent the parts of us that feel secure, avoidant, anxious-ambivalent, or disorganized. Here is Sara's attachment pie:

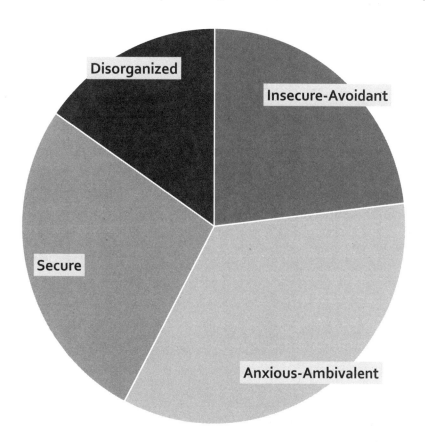

Take some time to write about your experience of attachment.

What do you know about your mother's pregnancy with you? Were there any significant stressors at that time? What do you notice in your body as you reflect on this question?

_____

_____

_____

Who were your primary caregivers after birth? Do you know if they were a source of positive connection and calming presence, or if they were dysregulating for you?

_____

_____

_____

As you read about attachment, do you relate strongly to any of the attachment styles? If so, which ones? How do those attachment styles show up in your current relationships?

_____

_____

_____

_____

_____

Create a pie that represents your own attachment tendencies. What percentage of the time in a week do you feel calm, at ease, and secure within yourself and your relationships? Represent that secure feeling with a section of your pie chart. Are there times you feel anxious in relationships and fearful of abandonment or rejection? What percentage of your pie would represent being anxious or ambivalent about relationships? How often in a week do you withdraw from connection or feel disconnected from your emotions? Draw the percentage of time that you feel insecure and avoidant. Last, are there times when you lash out at others or aggressively push away people that you love? Show the times that you feel disorganized in your pie. Remember to be gentle with yourself—all of these feelings are part of the complicated dance of attachment. Keep in mind that as you heal, you can increase your access to a felt sense of security. The percentage of your pie that represents secure attachment can and will grow over time.

Regulation in Relationship

As we discussed, your nervous system can become dysregulated from excessive sympathetic activation, which can lead you to feel restless, agitated, anxious, angry, or rageful. Additionally, your nervous system can become dysregulated through the dorsal vagal response to threat, which can lead you to feel fatigued, shut down, depressed, hopeless, dizzy, disconnected, or nauseous.

When you have a regulated nervous system, you are more likely to feel calm, connected, and clearheaded. However, *regulation* is a funny word. It seems to imply that you have everything under control. I'd like to invite you think of nervous system regulation as more of a dynamic process that allows you to respond effectively and lovingly to yourself and the world without needing to feel in control. Trying to manage yourself and others is not only exhausting, but also tends to backfire. Most of us do not like feeling controlled. We want to feel accepted for who we are. Emotions are by nature messy and vulnerable. Healing relationships allow you to feel seen and cared for by a trustworthy person who accepts you, mess and all.

When a child is hurt and we tell them not to cry, they learn to hold their pain inside, but this doesn't help them find resolution or regulation. In contrast, we attend to the child's pain by acknowledging the hurt they feel. Then, they might cry for a little while, but eventually the feeling will pass. If the child is really angry and having a tantrum, the caring parent helps them feel safe with those big feelings by providing a larger container—a person or space big enough to hold all of those emotions. Imagine a pitcher full of water. If you try and pour all of the water into a small glass, it will overflow. But if you pour the water into a large bowl, the water is held. Likewise, when a parent feels overwhelmed by a child's big feelings, they could go outside where the child can run around or put on music so the child can dance to move that big energy out of their body. So, a regulated nervous system is not the result of excessive control over your experience. Rather, it is the result of having someone who can be present with you and help you create safety in the midst of big feelings.

Coregulation allows a child to experience a felt sense of completion and inner calm. Parents or caregivers who provide these nurturing and protective spaces ultimately help the child recognize that their pain is tolerable and will pass. As children grow up, they internalize the compassionate messages received from their parents or caregivers, which helps them form a self-accepting and emotionally trusting internal dialogue.

Who has been a source of coregulation for you? Can you identify people in your life with whom you have felt safe and fully accepted? What do you notice in your body now as you think about these sources of support and care?

_____

_____

_____

If your traumatic events began in childhood, it is very likely that you did not have a coregulating environment. Instead of providing a respite from the stressors of the world, your parents or caregivers may have been a source of trauma. Write about what dysregulation looks like for you. Do you tend to be more anxious, agitated, or angry? Do you tend to feel shut down, fatigued, or depressed? Are you prone to taking care of others while simultaneously abandoning yourself?

_____

_____

_____

_____

_____

Even if you did not have coregulating relationships then, you can cultivate them now. However, when you have experienced relational trauma, perceiving people as sources of safety can be much harder to achieve. You might fear further rejection, criticism, abandonment, or abuse. Relational trauma can lead you to rely on self-defensive and protective strategies when your need for connection arises. This can lead you to feel caught between your need for safe and loving relationships on the one hand, and your learned survival response to withdraw from people on the other.

It is also common to sacrifice your own needs to uphold a relationship. For example, you might take care of others while ignoring yourself. This is often referred to as an *appeasement response* (Bailey et al. 2023). You might believe that if you take care of others, they will finally take care of you. Or, in some cases, you may have needed to take care of others in hopes that it would prevent them from hurting you. Not only can appeasement occur within family relationships, but this response can also arise as a strategy to navigate unsafe social and community spaces. For example, if you are discriminated against because of the color of your skin, you might need to be attentive to the needs of people in power to ensure that they do not perceive you as a threat. When left unresolved, these relational patterns can leave you stuck feeling untethered, ungrounded, and disconnected—even from yourself. This too is a symptom of trauma. When nothing you do works to create safety, you might have to rely on a *fawn response*, in which you submit to the demands of another for the purpose of survival (Walker 2013).

We all have natural rhythms that underlie our needs for connection and disconnection. Honoring these rhythms is part of the healing journey. For example, you might notice times when you want to make eye contact and times when you feel an urge to look away or close your eyes. When you give yourself permission to shift your attention internally, you are better able to sense yourself and your own needs. Then, you can honor when you are ready to come back into connection with another person while still remaining connected to yourself. Doing so helps you set boundaries and stop patterns of over-giving or self-sacrifice. Take some time to reflect on your rhythms of connection and separateness in relationships:

What are your tendencies in relationships? Do you notice times that you withdraw from connection, even though you really want to be close? Are there times when you have taken care of others, but felt like you ignored your own needs?

How do your rhythms of connection and disconnection show up in your relationships? What signals let you know that you want to be in connection? What cues let you know that you need to take space or bring your attention inward?

_____

_____

_____

_____

Imagine how it will feel to have relationships with others while simultaneously feeling a deep connection to yourself. What would you like to do differently to help create nourishing relationships in your life now?

_____

_____

_____

_____

Coregulation can happen in many ways, and it does not always require other people. Some of us find it easier to cultivate a sense of connection to pets, music, or special places in nature. We can also find coregulating activities such as drumming, dancing, or moving our body in a yoga practice. Coregulation can occur in any environment or during any activity that brings you back to the essential rhythms of yourself. For example, imagine walking on the beach as you feel the warm sun on your skin, the scent of salt in the air, and the feeling of the sand under your bare feet. Or, you might prefer to imagine snuggling with a pet on the couch in the comfort of your home. Whatever image is nourishing for you, notice how your body responds.

Remember that the outcome of a good coregulating experience is that you feel more connected to yourself and able to turn toward your emotions with greater compassion and acceptance. As a result, you are more likely to feel calm and capable of responding well to everyday stressful events, such as getting stuck in traffic.

Identify sources of coregulation that you can connect to on a regular basis that do not include other people. You might think of pets or special places that feel peaceful and nourishing. Also think about activities that help you feel a greater sense of connection to yourself, such as walking outdoors, dancing, journaling, or meditating. Write down a list of these external sources of coregulation.

_____

_____

_____

_____

_____

Cultivating a Loving Relationship with Yourself

The coregulating relationships in your life strengthen an invisible internal wiring within your nervous system that helps you to hold yourself lovingly. Therefore, we tend to think of coregulation as a precursor to *self-regulation*. Self-regulation is cultivated when you reduce unnecessary suffering related to your painful emotions. The goal is not to get rid of your feelings, but rather to observe your emotions with compassion and acceptance, without jumping into reactivity or behaviors that might be harmful. Healing from trauma involves cultivating a deep sense of connection with yourself. You do so when you turn toward yourself in a loving and compassionate manner.

When you have a history of trauma, it is common to internalize critical or disparaging messages toward yourself, which can develop into negative beliefs about yourself. For example, you might believe that you are unworthy, unlovable, weak, or broken. These negative beliefs interfere with your ability to know that you deserve to be loved, supported, and treated with respect. Reclaiming a loving internal voice invites you to notice unhelpful narratives and revise the ways that you speak to yourself.

EXERCISE
Positive and Negative Beliefs

Take a look at this list of negative beliefs that commonly arise when you have a history of trauma. Do any of these beliefs arise for you? Circle the ones that do, then write about what seems to trigger these thoughts.

I am not enough.

I am unworthy.

I am unlovable.

I am weak.

I am bad.

I am broken.

It is my fault.

I am helpless and powerless to change my circumstances.

I cannot trust myself.

I cannot trust anyone.

I have to be perfect in order to be loved.

_____

_____

_____

_____

_____

_____

Now, I invite you to look at this list of reparative, positive beliefs that can generate greater kindness toward yourself. Put a star next to any that you would like to strengthen as a foundation of self-compassion. Write down any other positive beliefs that aren't on this list that you would like to strengthen.

I am good enough just as I am.

I am worthy and deserving of... (love, kindness, respect, etc.).

I am lovable.

I am strong.

I am a good person.

I am whole.

It was not my fault.

I have choices now that can support me to create a healthy and meaningful life.

I can learn to trust myself.

I can choose who to trust.

I am human and can learn from my mistakes.

I can love and accept myself just as I am.

_____

_____

_____

_____

_____

_____

Loving-kindness and compassion-based practices are associated with an increase in the healthy tone of your vagus nerve and greater positive emotions, along with reductions in symptoms of PTSD, depression, and anxiety (Phillips and Hine 2021). The next practice will gently guide you through this concept of holding yourself in a loving manner. You can think of self-compassion as an act of friendliness toward yourself, in which you practice extending kindness toward yourself through your words and actions.

Regrettably, if you have a history of trauma, it is often difficult to turn toward yourself in a loving manner. Sometimes, the invitation to bring in self-compassion leads to an increase in self-criticism, along with distressing emotions or an increase in physical tension. If you find it difficult to accept yourself, see if you can become curious about your experience. When vulnerable emotions arise, explore what additional support you might need in order to be present with your feelings. Explore this process for yourself.

EXERCISE
Self-Compassion Meditation

You can practice this as a guided meditation by listening to the audio track available at http://www.newharbinger.com/54162.

Find a comfortable seat as you prepare yourself for this self-compassion practice. Notice your state of mind, body, and any emotions that are present for you at this time. When you have a history of unresolved trauma, it is common to feel as though there is something wrong with you—as if you are flawed, broken, or unworthy of love. Those are the misguided beliefs fueled by shame and the wounds of your past. I am here to assure you that no matter what you have experienced in the past, you deserve your own care, kindness, and compassion.

Even though part of you might feel unworthy or ashamed, can you sense that there is also a part of you that feels worthy of care? Recognize the part of you that is courageously showing up for yourself right now, and notice how it feels to offer yourself loving-kindness in this moment. You do not need to push away difficult feelings or thoughts. Rather, try to be present with whatever you are feeling today and to simultaneously know that you deserve care, kindness, and compassion. It might not feel totally believable yet, but even the intention to hold yourself lovingly is a powerful step toward healing.

If you find it difficult to turn toward yourself with kindness, it can be helpful to imagine how a kind and loving person would speak to you if they knew the pain you were feeling. Or, you can imagine another person who is experiencing a similar kind of pain and how you might comfort them. Once you've imagined that, notice if it feels easier to turn toward yourself in a loving manner.

I invite you to recognize that healing doesn't happen all at once. It is a slow and steady process. You can return to this practice as often as you would like, knowing that over time, you will begin to feel stronger and more deserving. Self-compassion will become easier with repeated practice. Take a moment to honor your courage and commitment to showing up for yourself with kindness today.

It is powerful to explore self-compassion as a body-centered practice. You can do so by placing your hands over your head, throat, chest, or belly. In general, touch has been shown to reduce stress hormones, heart rate, and blood pressure while increasing the feel-good neurochemicals of oxytocin, gamma-aminobutyric acid (GABA), and serotonin (Truitt 2022). These hormones and neurotransmitters are associated with enhanced tone of the vagus nerve and inhibition of the sympathetic nervous system. They are also the same chemicals that are released when babies feel safe and loved by their caregivers.

Self-applied touch can be thought of as a loving way to reparent yourself—you are giving your body the felt experience of bonding now, even if you did not have that in childhood (Gothard and Fuglevand 2022). Keep in mind that your head, throat, heart, and belly are all areas where your vagus nerve travels through your body. When you place your hands in each location, you are gently supporting your physical and emotional well-being.

In the next set of practices, try strengthening affirming beliefs about yourself while engaging in an embodied self-compassion exercise. These practices are simple yet powerful body-centered ways to anchor a felt sense of connection to yourself and strengthen self-acceptance, loving-kindness, and self-compassion. You can do some or all of these practices, and adapt them so that they feel comfortable for you. These practices are a lovely way to offer loving-kindness to yourself first thing in the morning as a daily practice. Begin exploring these practices in moments of ease and calm to build your capacity with self-compassion. Once you feel comfortable with the practices, start to use them during moments of emotional distress and experiment with these self-soothing statements. Over time, you might discover that you are automatically drawn to self-applied touch and accompanying statements of self-acceptance. With repeated practice, embodied self-compassion simply becomes a part of your everyday life.

EXERCISE
Embodied Self-Compassion Practice

You can listen to the audio track of this guided practice available at http://www.newharbinger.com/54162.

Practice 1: Place your hands around your cheeks as you allow your face to rest in your palms. While holding your head in your hands, quietly say to yourself, "Even though I sometimes have negative or self-critical thoughts, I am willing to generate loving and kind thoughts toward myself." Repeat these words two more times while holding yourself.

Practice 2: Place your hands gently along the sides of your neck, so that the heels of your palms come together in front of your chin. With your hands lightly placed over your throat, quietly say to yourself, "Even though I feel hurt, I can acknowledge these feelings while being gentle with myself." Repeat these words two more times while gently supporting your neck and throat with your hands.

Practice 3: Place your hands over your heart, one palm over the other. Then, quietly say to yourself, "Even though I sometimes feel unworthy or unlovable, I recognize that all people including myself deserve compassion, love, and support." Repeat these words two more times while holding your heart.

Practice 4: Place both hands on your belly, over your navel or wherever feels right for you. Then, quietly say to yourself, "Even though I sometimes feel broken, weak, and powerless, I recognize the strength and courage it takes to build compassion for my pain." Repeat these words two more times while resting your hands on your belly.

Practice 5: Offer yourself an experience of holding yourself, like a hug, by placing each hand on the opposite shoulder. While hugging yourself, sense your breath as you quietly say to yourself, "With each breath, I grow in my ability to love and accept myself just as I am. As I receive this kindness and compassion, I reclaim my ability to sense myself as healthy and whole, one breath at a time." Sense your breath moving in and out of your heart as you repeat these words two more times.

As you finish these practices, what are you aware of? Were any of these practices or statements of self-compassion challenging? If so, what would support you as you navigate your own barriers to self-compassion?

_____

_____

_____

_____

_____

_____

_____

Building Your Capacity to Cultivate Nourishing Relationships

As you strengthen your ability to hold yourself with love, you may feel more capable of being a coregulator for other people. Rather than being dysregulated by another person's distress, you are able to offer your soothing and caring presence. Simply put, when you are able to deeply love and accept yourself, you are better able to show up for others in a loving manner. You can learn to cultivate positive attachment relationships at any stage of your life. Even if you did not have a secure attachment relationship in childhood, you can cultivate positive attachment, bonding experiences, and coregulating relationships now. This allows you to tap into the life-changing power of love. The key question is how do you cultivate the ABCs of connection in your life now? There are some predictable steps that can help.

- **Cultivate self-awareness:** Research suggests that knowing your attachment history and relationship patterns is a precursor to change (Siegel 2010). You have already begun this step by exploring your past. Additionally, pay attention to your current relationships and how you tend to show up. Get to know any habitual beliefs about yourself that might be interfering with your ability to give and receive love.

- **Look for trustworthy companions:** Not everyone will meet your needs or be worthy of your trust. But there are many people out there who are kind and reliable. Seek out people who prove they are trustworthy. These individuals will follow through on their commitments and show up in a dependable and supportive manner. It is equally important that you learn to be this trustworthy companion, too.

- **Foster healthy communication:** You can learn a lot about yourself by noticing how you react to others and how you communicate your needs. You foster healthy communication when you practice listening to others with an intention to understand their perspective. Criticism interferes with emotional safety. Practice setting your judgments aside and listening with an intention to offer support. Additionally, you promote positive experiences of bonding when you are willing to be vulnerable by expressing your feelings and asking for what you need.

- **Practice setting boundaries:** If you find yourself in relationship with someone who is not treating you with respect, dignity, and kindness, then it is likely important for you to set a boundary. Boundaries begin with knowing your limits and validating your needs. Boundaries do not need to be an absolute cutoff, although if someone is hurting you, this may be necessary. More often, boundaries are an opportunity for you to assert your expectations about how you want to be treated. If another person is incapable of respecting you, then you might decide to find someone else who can.

Take some time to reflect on your relationship to others in your life now. Do you have sources of secure attachment in your life now? If so, write down any people who provide you with reliable and consistent care, compassion, and kindness. How do you feel in your body as you think about these positive connections?

_____

_____

_____

_____

_____

_____

_____

_____

_____

_____

In what ways can you offer coregulation to others? What emotions arise for you now as you reflect on providing your compassionate presence to another? How do you feel in your body now?

While the people in your life do not need to be perfect, are they generally able to respond to you respectfully and kindly? Are they willing to make amends when they have caused you harm? If not, how might you benefit from setting clearer boundaries and expectations about how you want to be treated?

_____

_____

_____

_____

_____

_____

_____

Cultivating nourishing relationships involves skills that require repeated practice and patience. It is normal to feel frustrated with the messiness of human relationships, especially when you feel rejected or have hurt a loved one's feelings. These are key moments to return to the self-compassion practices and know that you do not need to be perfect to be loved. In time, your capacity to receive and give the gift of connection will grow stronger.

CHAPTER 3

Rewiring Your Brain for Resilience

Being human involves inevitable exposure to stress, and research suggests that most of us will be exposed to at least one traumatic event in our lifetimes. These challenging life events tend to take a toll on our physical and mental well-being. You might notice your own tendencies to feel anxious and irritable, or shut down with fatigue and depression. Stress and trauma can also have detrimental impacts on your physical health, leading to a wide range of illnesses and chronic pain symptoms, including migraines, asthma, digestive issues, chronic fatigue syndrome, fibromyalgia, autoimmune conditions, and more.

When we look at the root cause of these symptoms, we see that they are associated with the dysregulation of the autonomic nervous system (Gazerani and Cairns 2018; Martins et al. 2021; Rasmussen et al. 2018). As you have learned, the autonomic nervous system is made up of two branches: the sympathetic and the parasympathetic. When your nervous system is out of balance, one of these systems is dominant, leading you to either be keyed up in fight or flight or in a state of collapse and exhaustion. You might even alternate between these extreme states.

Your autonomic nervous system is regulated by your vagus nerve. High *vagal tone* is a key to maintaining a healthy body and mind. Vagal tone refers to being able to transition smoothly between sympathetic and parasympathetic states, which allows you to resiliently respond to everyday challenges. As we discussed in chapter 2, the vagus nerve can be thought of as a mind-body superhighway of communication that helps your nervous system come into balance.

Whether you feel stressed and tense, or collapsed with fatigue, it is possible to return to a place of greater ease and a deeper connection to yourself. You can do so through stimulation of the vagus nerve with practices that have been demonstrated to increase vagal tone. These practices help rewire your body and mind into greater states of resilience. Your vagus nerve has nerve fibers that innervate your lungs, heart, and digestive organs. When you stimulate your vagus nerve, you are also enhancing the health of your whole body, including the functioning of your respiratory, cardiovascular, digestive, endocrine, and immune systems.

As a result of vagal stimulation practices, most people immediately feel a shift. You might notice an increased awareness of your body sensations or emotions, which can feel little uncomfortable at first. However, over time and with practice, most people begin to notice a greater feeling of ease, connection, and inner peace. This is because the vagus nerve unites your mind and body, allowing you to sense a deep connection to your innermost self.

In this chapter, you will learn about your enteric nervous system and how your vagus nerve works with this "belly brain" to help you feel connected to your instincts as a source of intuition and inner wisdom. You will discover the power of positive neuroplasticity and how this can rewire your brain to be more resilient to the inevitable stressors that we all face as part of being human. I will then guide you through several vagus nerve stimulation practices to help show how simple daily practices can help you create greater balance. Finally, I empower you to create a routine that will help you bring rhythms of regulation into your daily life.

Accessing the Wisdom of Your Belly Brain

Your vagus nerve is deeply interconnected with all of your digestive organs, including your stomach, intestines, spleen, liver, and pancreas. Your digestive organs make up your *enteric nervous system*, which is often referred to as your "belly brain" because your gut produces the same neurotransmitters (e.g., serotonin and dopamine) found in your brain.

In addition, we all have a gut microbiome—which consists of bacteria and other micro-organisms—that works with our immune system to help keep our body healthy. There is a strong connection between your digestive system and nervous system, called the *gut-brain axis*. Your vagus nerve provides bidirectional communication between the two. Simply put, when you are anxious, your gut is more likely to become dysregulated, and when your gut microbiome is out of balance, you are more likely to feel anxious.

Moreover, there is a correlation between having lower vagal tone and digestive conditions such as irritable bowel syndrome (IBS) and inflammatory bowel disease (IBD) (Bonaz, Bazin, and Pellissier 2018). For example, you might notice that when you travel, you might be more likely to become constipated, or that a stressful event leads to a flare-up of IBS symptoms. While you might feel embarrassed by or even ashamed of these experiences, it is also important to recognize that gut imbalances are extremely common when you have a trauma history.

I would like to invite you to think of your digestive system as profoundly intelligent. Your gut helps you navigate the world by allowing you to discern nourishing experiences from those that are unhealthy. When you eat, your digestive system functions to differentiate nutrients from waste, and if you have eaten food that has gone bad, such as with food poisoning, your gut wisely rejects the toxins.

Your belly brain also helps you digest all of your life experiences, including what you take in from movies, social media, and exchanges you have with other people. You might notice that you have instinctual reactions to your life experiences. For example, you can sense what feels good or nourishing because your belly feels soft and your body feels relaxed. Your body also gives you feedback about experiences that feel unkind or threatening. You might feel a knot in your belly, tension in your muscles, or a general sense of discomfort throughout your body.

Explore your stress response: Think of a difficult moment. Perhaps you had a conflict with a loved one or received a hurtful text. What emotions arise? How does your body respond?

_____

_____

_____

_____

_____

_____

Notice your relaxation response: Think of a positive or nourishing experience. For example, a time when you felt heard and understood by another person. What do you notice now? Again, pay attention to how your body responds when you think of this moment.

_____

_____

_____

_____

_____

_____

If you have a history of trauma, you may have had to disconnect from your gut feelings as a coping mechanism. For example, if you grew up in an unsafe home, you may have had to dissociate from your bodily felt sense. This is especially true if you experienced ongoing abuse or neglect. Remaining disconnected from your body can lead to a profound sense of confusion, as it leaves you cut off from your instinctual self. You might even find it difficult to distinguish between what is nourishing and what is harmful. For example, you might eat a meal but not sense that you are full. Or you might enter into a hurtful relationship without paying attention to your body's signals that you feel unsafe.

Practices that stimulate your vagus nerve help you reclaim awareness of the felt self of your body. You begin to identify that your body is saying "no" when you feel tense, uneasy, repulsed, or disgusted. You also begin to see how your body says "yes" by paying attention to what feels good, nourishing, and easeful. Once you can feel your body, you can use this information to help make decisions or clarify your boundaries. Doing so allows you to reorient your life based on your body's inner compass, which is always with you. It becomes easier to know when you need to set a boundary and protect yourself, and when it is safe to open your heart to those who are trustworthy. Most importantly, you rebuild trust in yourself as you learn to listen to your inner voice, or your instinctual self, which speaks in sensations rather than in words.

Do you sometimes feel disconnected from your body? If so, how might this be related to your past? Remember, dissociating from your felt sense may have been an intelligent way for you to navigate difficult experiences. Try to feel compassion toward yourself.

_____

_____

_____

_____

_____

_____

_____

Are there times that you feel connected to your body? When do you feel more embodied? What activities enhance this connection?

_____

_____

_____

_____

_____

_____

_____

The Power of Positive Neuroplasticity

The science of *neuroplasticity* teaches that our brains change with every life experience, and that we are capable of growth throughout our lifespan. Within your brain, you have approximately eighty-six billion interconnected neurons. All your life experiences, memories, beliefs, emotions, and behaviors are encoded as networks of connectivity between your neurons. Hebb's law is a scientific principle that explains that the neurons that fire together will also wire together (Siegel 1999). Whatever you repeatedly think, feel, or sense is going to either build new or strengthen existing patterns of neural connection in your brain.

Neuroplasticity can facilitate your growth in the direction of positive states, but it can also strengthen negative states, difficult emotions, or negative beliefs about yourself. From this perspective, you can think of PTSD as a form of *stress-induced neuroplasticity* (Deppermann et al. 2014). For example, fear-based networks in your brain are reinforced when you are repeatedly flooded by reexperiencing symptoms, such as worst-case scenario thinking, flashbacks, and difficult emotions. Very often, traumatic events can cause you to feel stuck ruminating about the past or worrying excessively about the future. When you have painful emotions and memories, you can often get caught in a downward spiral in which you selectively recall times when you felt hopeless, rejected, or alone.

When healing from trauma, it is important to learn how to find relief from these looping thoughts and emotional states. This doesn't mean that you ignore your pain; however, it's important to interrupt these repetitive negative states and reorient your attention to an experience of safety and connection. Once you have cultivated a felt sense of ease, you will feel more capable of turning toward your own hurt with compassion. Doing so allows you to heal the pain rather than feel stuck inside it. All of the exercises in this book aim to help you learn to turn toward your pain with compassion, which lets you simultaneously recognize your struggles and your strength. This begins the process of building positive neuroplasticity, which involves purposefully and intentionally changing your neural networks in a wanted direction.

Because our nervous system is hardwired to protect us, we register cues of threats within a fraction of a second. It doesn't take long for the nervous system to react to any hint of danger—even if we have not consciously registered the threat. Your nervous system can move into a state of threat response very quickly in response to the tone of someone's voice, an expression on their face, an image on social media, or a story in the news. In response, your heart rate might increase or your breath might quicken. In contrast, when building conscious awareness of a positive state, it often takes closer to twenty or thirty seconds for your nervous system to register the cues of safety and for your body to respond (Hanson 2016).

When you are purposefully changing or growing neural networks, you need to do so with directed effort. Neuroplastic change requires that you inhibit habitual negative thinking patterns and redirect your attention toward anything that enhances a positive feeling in your body (Ogden and Fisher 2015). The practices in this book guide you to enhance positive changes as you engage beneficial thinking patterns, visualize times when you have felt safe, and perform an embodiment practice that feel nourishing. Neuroplasticity is supported by repeated practice. Therefore, the work becomes repeating the new behavior again and again.

Perhaps you can remember learning to tie your shoes or ride a bike. The first time, it was awkward. You might have even felt frustrated for a while, but eventually, because of repeated practice, you learned a new skill. Now, you don't have to think about it anymore. When healing from your trauma, you are building new neural networks of positive states in your brain, but eventually, the experience of nourishment and ease comes more naturally and without effort.

When healing from trauma, it is wise to begin with building your capacity to sustain *positive resource states*. The word *resource* refers to any current experience or memory of positive states, such as moments when you feel or have felt safe, loved, comforted, protected, competent, empowered, peaceful, or relaxed. These positive states release natural feel-good chemicals such as dopamine, oxytocin, serotonin, and endorphins. Through repeated practice, you strengthen the neural networks associated with these states. You might even notice that once you recall one positive memory, it becomes easier to identify other times when you have felt that same way. Now, you are finding an upward spiral of positive emotions (Kok and Fredrickson 2010).

Sometimes it is challenging to find a positive state. In this case, it may feel more accessible to find a neutral state of being "okay," which can still help interrupt the looping of worries or negative thinking patterns. As you build your resources, you will be able to attend to your pain without feeling like it's going to take over. You are setting the foundation to attend to your suffering wisely.

After learning about neuroplasticity, do you notice thinking patterns that are rooted in the traumatic events of your past? Are you aware of any looping thoughts that initiate a downward spiral of negative memories, thoughts, and emotions?

_____

_____

_____

_____

_____

_____

_____

Practice shifting out of this state. You can build positive neuroplasticity by writing on the lines below about a time when you felt safe, loved, comforted, protected, competent, empowered, peaceful, or relaxed. Pause and savor any positive emotions as you write about this experience.

_____

_____

_____

_____

Now, identify any thoughts that produce a more beneficial response. What would you like to tell yourself now? What thoughts generate feelings of hope, courage, or strength within you?

_____

_____

_____

_____

_____

_____

_____

_____

Rewire Your Resilience with Natural Vagus Nerve Stimulation

Treatments for post-traumatic stress tend to be most effective when they offer psychological and sensory-based interventions that help us work with the mental, emotional, and physiological factors that worsen symptoms (Ruden 2019). This supports you in creating changes in how your think about yourself, while also changing how your feel in your body by adding sensory input that helps you feel more easeful and connected to yourself.

One of the most direct ways to attend to the dysregulation of the autonomic nervous system is through vagus nerve stimulation. Vagus nerve stimulation has been found to reduce the intensity of and frequency of symptoms of anxiety, depression, migraines, fibromyalgia, rheumatoid arthritis, lupus, and inflammatory bowel disease (Bonaz et al. 2021; Molero-Chamizo et al. 2022; Ramkissoon et al. 2021; Rasmussen et al. 2018).

Initially, vagus nerve stimulation was delivered through bioelectronic devices that were surgically implanted—like a pacemaker—and sent imperceptible impulses to the vagus nerve. Now, we know that noninvasive devices can also successfully stimulate the vagus nerve in areas of the body where it travels close to the surface of the skin, such as on the sides or back of the neck, and on areas surrounding the ear. You can also naturally stimulate your vagus nerve through the use of cold immersion, conscious breathing, self-applied touch, eye movements, yoga, tai chi, gratitude practices, self-compassion, and meditation (Goggins et al. 2022; Kok et al. 2013; Magnon et al. 2021; Zou et al. 2018).

Another term for vagus nerve stimulation is *neuromodulation*, or nervous system change. I invite you to think of the process as a gentle awakening of the ventral vagal circuit—your social engagement system—in a manner that is both soothing and enlivening. Think of your vagus nerve as a large river that begins at your brainstem, with channels that extend upward toward your face and downward through your neck, heart, and lungs, with a final destination in your digestive and reproductive organs. Just like any river, if the flow is impeded in one area, it will impact the entire channel. When you engage in vagus nerve stimulation practices, you are opening the flow of this river.

Most importantly, practices that engage vagus nerve stimulation are easy to incorporate into a daily routine, only requiring about ten minutes once or twice a day. These practices are both affordable and accessible, and when you do them daily, you are using the power of positive neuroplasticity to rewire your resilience.

I invite you begin with the following practices, which aim to soothe and support your nervous system. Between each exercise, I encourage you to pause, reflect, and write about your experience using the lines after the exercise.

EXERCISE
Cold Water Exposure and the Diving Reflex

Simply splashing cold water on your face—from your lips to your scalp line—stimulates the diving reflex. The diving reflex tends to slow your heart rate, increase blood flow to your brain, reduce anger, and relax your body (Al Haddad et al. 2010). You can also achieve these nervous system cooling effects by placing ice cubes in a plastic bag and holding the ice against your face while briefly holding your breath.

_____

_____

_____

_____

_____

_____

_____

EXERCISE
Valsalva Maneuver

The Valsalva maneuver stimulates the vagus nerve by attempting to exhale against a closed airway. This creates temporary pressure inside of your chest cavity, which enhances vagal tone (Chen et al. 2020; Mailk et al. 2018). Due to the pressure it creates, it is not recommended if you have a detached retina or lens implants in your eyes, and should be used with caution if you have coronary artery disease or congenital heart disease. If you would like to try this practice, take a deep breath, then keep your mouth closed and pinch your nose while trying to breathe out.

_____

_____

_____

_____

_____

_____

_____

EXERCISE
Vagus Nerve Stimulation Practices

You can explore this guided practice by listening to the audio track available at http://www
.newharbinger.com/54162.

Self-Applied Massage to Your Face

The upper circuits of the ventral vagus nerve work closely with other cranial nerves, such as
your trigeminal nerve and facial nerves, which are responsible for the sensations in your face
and your ability to express emotions. Applying a gentle massage to areas of your face where
these nerves come close to the surface of your face is another way to gently stimulate the vagus
nerve (Fazeli et al. 2016). Embedded within the skin of your face are specialized nerve cells that
are sensitive to touch called *c-tactile fibers*. Stimulating these fibers through light touch helps
reduce your heart rate, reduce pain, and increase positive emotions (Schirmer et al. 2023; Truitt
2022). To explore this practice:

1. Place your fingertips at the center of your forehead and gently sweep them outward
   toward your temples. You can allow this movement to feel intuitive.

2. Perhaps pause for a moment in the space between your eyebrows with gentle circular movements.

3. You might also create circular movements around your temples.

4. Next, place your fingertips by the bridge of your nose and find sweeping movements along the tops of your cheekbones, outward toward your temples. Follow any
   intuitive movements that feel nourishing to you.

5. Last, place your fingertips by the bridge of your nose and create sweeping movements under your cheekbones, outward toward your ears.

6. Continue with these movements for as long as you would like, noticing the sensations in your face, along with any other sensations or emotions that you are aware
   of in your body.

Self-Applied Massage to Your Ears

The ears are a common location for vagus nerve stimulation because there are high amounts of vagal fibers running through specific areas of your ear. These areas are called the tragus, the area of cartilage just in front of your ear canal, and the concha, which surrounds your ear canal. You can practice on both sides at once or one ear at a time.

1. Locate the tragus (see illustration) and place your thumb behind and pointer finger in front while gently squeezing this area of your ear.

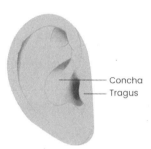

2. Continue this gentle contact to your ears for about one minute, pressing and massaging.

3. Take the tip of your finger and move it around on the concha.

4. Explore these movements intuitively.

5. You might also explore rolling your earlobes between your thumbs and first fingers. This should feel good.

6. Another gentle release for your ears involves placing your middle finger in front of your ear and your pointer finger behind your ear, as you gently massage those areas. This can also offer a gentle release for the muscles of your jaw. Continue for another minute or two as you notice any subtle changes, such as a feeling of warmth or relaxation in your ears, face, or body.

Self-Applied Massage to Your Neck

Your vagus nerve passes through your neck alongside your carotid artery and sits only one and a half centimeters under your skin. Massage therapy has demonstrated effects on improving vagal tone, and you can gain the same benefits through a self-applied vagus nerve massage (Meier et al. 2020). To explore this practice:

1. Place your fingertips at the back of your skull, underneath the occipital ridge, at the top of your neck.

2. With circular movements, begin to move your hands forward until they are under your ears, near your jawbone.

3. Continue to create circular movements with your fingertips as you move your hands downward along the sides of your neck.

4. You do not need to apply deep pressure for the massage to be effective. While you can continue for as long as you would like, even one to two minutes is beneficial.

The remaining chapters of this workbook deepen this journey with vagus nerve stimulation techniques facilitated by conscious breathing, bilateral integration strategies, mindful movements, and relaxation techniques. Rewiring your resilience relies on repetition. Just like learning to ride your bike or tie your shoes, as you practice vagus nerve stimulation within a daily routine, you will notice that it becomes easier to access a felt sense of balance within your nervous system.

CHAPTER 4

Conscious Breathing to Enhance the Body-Mind Connection

Your breath is an essential part of your autonomic nervous system. Changes in how you are breathing are also one of the first signs that you are feeling threatened. You might begin to breathe rapidly into your upper chest, breathe shallowly, or unconsciously hold your breath. Breathing rapidly is part of your sympathetic nervous system response, to help you flee from or fight off danger. While these reactions to stressful or traumatic events may serve a purpose in times of difficulty, we sometimes engage in inefficient or stress-inducing breath patterns well after an event has subsided. In this case, you might notice lingering patterns of muscular tension in your chest and shoulders, or feelings of ongoing anxiety and panic. In contrast, shallow breathing is part of the dorsal vagal expression of the parasympathetic nervous system. Over time, shallow breathing might lead you to feel lethargic, fatigued, or disconnected from your body. In either case, your body and brain will continue to remain in a threat response, which can deplete your overall sense of joy and well-being.

When it comes to nervous system regulation, your breath is the fastest way to cultivate balance. This is because the breath can be under both automatic and volitional control. Your autonomic nervous system allows you to breathe without requiring any awareness on your part. However, your volitional nervous system lets you choose when and how to engage in conscious breathing practices. For example, you can practice altering the pace and rhythm of your breath as a way to purposefully regulate your nervous system. Every inhalation stimulates your sympathetic nervous system, and every exhalation initiates a parasympathetic nervous system response. When you engage slow inhalations and exhalations that are same length, you cultivate a balanced physiological state that can help you feel both attentive and at ease. When you emphasize your exhale, you will engage a greater parasympathetic response and a deeper sense of calm. Conversely, you can also choose to emphasize your inhale to engage your sympathetic system. When you are not in a state of threat, this energizing breath supports you to play, exercise, feel motivated, or find a sense of excitement about your life.

When you feel safe, the muscles of your abdomen and diaphragm tend to relax, which allows for the satisfying feeling of a deep belly breath. In contrast, chronic physical tension around your abdomen, diaphragm, and ribcage tends to restrict the flow of breath. These tension patterns can arise as a result of chronic stress or traumatic life events. As you learn to breathe consciously, you might begin to notice these restrictive tendencies in your body. Such awareness allows you to engage in mindful movements, which help unwind tension patterns in your body and can help you find a deeper, fuller breath.

Within this chapter, you will learn the science of conscious breathing and how it is deeply connected to the tone of your vagus nerve. You will learn about the fascia that surround your abdomen, diaphragm, rib cage, heart, and lungs, and how breathing fully helps you find greater emotional freedom. I will guide you through several conscious breathing practices aimed to help tap into your innate resilience. Read on to discover how your body, mind, and breath are intricately connected, and why conscious breathing helps you tap into an inner source of strength and courage.

Breathing and Your Emotions

When you have a history of trauma, conscious breathing can feel uncomfortable. If this is the case for you, please know that you are not alone. Your breath is deeply connected to your ability to feel your emotions. And healing from the traumatic events of your past involves feeling and expressing your vulnerable emotions. Initially, this might feel uncomfortable. You may have worked for years to avoid certain feelings. The invitation to explore conscious breathing might bring these emotions to the surface, and you might feel more discomfort before you find relief. You can pace yourself and support vulnerable emotions by returning to the practices that helped you orient to safety in chapter 1, the self-compassion strategies in chapter 2, or the natural vagus nerve stimulation interventions from chapter 3.

In truth, many of us resist feeling our emotions. This is especially true if our parents or primary caregivers were not able to respond to our emotions in a loving manner. Perhaps you were rejected, punished, shamed, or ignored when you expressed your feelings as a child. If so, you might have developed the belief that you are too much to handle or that being vulnerable is weak. Some cultural or societal groups also influence our emotional expression. For example, you may have received messages at home or in school that you need to be tough, or that crying and feeling afraid are signs of weakness. If nobody was ever able to compassionately relate to you when you were having strong emotions, you may have learned to cut off from your feelings as a coping strategy. This can leave you feeling numb and disconnected from yourself. Even if your parents, caregivers, or teachers were unable to respond in a caring manner to your emotions, you can learn to do so now.

If you have been frozen or numb, you might feel frightened when you start to thaw and you have access to your emotions again. As feelings arise, I invite you to imagine that they are like waves on the ocean. They are designed to come and go. They rise up, crest, release, and subside. You can learn to surf these waves. Take some time to reflect on your relationship to your breath and your emotions:

How has your relationship to your breath been shaped by past traumas?

_____

_____

_____

_____

_____

Do you tend to hold your breath? Do you notice if you breathe shallowly? Do you feel as though you can take a deep, full breath?

_____

_____

_____

What emotions, if any, arise for you when you focus on your breath?

_____

_____

_____

_____

What messages did you receive about your vulnerable emotions from your parents or caregivers? How were you treated as a child when you felt afraid, hurt, or sad? Were there other influential people or community spaces that shaped how you express your feelings? If so, what messages did you receive from them?

_____

_____

_____

_____

_____

_____

_____

What beliefs do you carry about expressing your emotions? Notice if any of the following beliefs arise for you. Are there any other beliefs not listed here that you notice? Can you sense where your core beliefs about emotions came from?

- *I won't be able to handle it if I feel my emotions.*

- *I am weak if I express my emotions.*

- *I am too much for others and I will be rejected if I show how I am really feeling.*

- *I'd like to be able to feel, but I am numb and this will never change.*

- _____

- _____

- _____

- _____

What new beliefs about expressing your emotions would you like to cultivate? Notice if any of the following statements resonate with you, or add your own new belief.

- *Even if others couldn't handle my emotions, I can learn to be with my feelings now.*

- *Expressing my emotions is a sign of strength and courage.*

- *Even if I was rejected in the past when I expressed my emotions, I can find people in my life now who show me respect and care when I am sad, afraid, or hurt.*

- *I can reclaim my ability to feel my emotions, as I connect to my body and breath.*

- _____

- _____

- _____

- _____

- _____

Over time, you will learn to trust that even big feelings resolve into a sense of relief or ease. After an emotional release, you are likely to feel more connected to yourself and to feel a greater sense of freedom.

The Anatomy of the Breath

As we begin to explore the breath, let's turn our attention to key structures in the anatomy of our breath—our lungs, heart, diaphragm, the intercostal muscles between our ribs, and our psoas muscles deep within our belly. Traumatic events can lead us to accumulate physical tension around these areas, which restricts the flow of the breath. The lungs, heart, diaphragm, and intercostal and psoas muscles are inextricably related to each other through the fascial web, which consists of layers of connective tissue that extend throughout your body.

Fascia has been described as the largest sensory organ in your body because it has approximately 250 million nerve endings, which work together to help you sense and feel (Schleip

2017). These connective tissues carry the neurotransmitters and hormones, such as serotonin, dopamine, GABA, and oxytocin, throughout your body. These neurochemicals form the basis of your emotions (Pert 1997). When you move and breathe, your fascia acts like a lubricating fluid in your body, supporting easeful movements and the flow of your emotions. In contrast, stress, trauma, and lack of movement can cause the fascia to become sticky or hardened, which is associated with greater fatigue, pain, inflammation, and immune system imbalances (Miller 2023). Throughout this book, you will find invitations for gentle movements that help nourish and hydrate your fascia.

The Diaphragm-Heart (Pericardium) Connection

Let's look more closely at the fascial connections between the areas of your body involved in the breath. The fascia of your diaphragm connects to the connective tissue around your heart, which is called the pericardium, also known as the heart protector in the Traditional Chinese Medicine system. When you inhale, the diaphragm is meant to lower and expand, which gently tugs on the pericardium, creating more space around your heart. On the exhalation, your diaphragm returns to its natural resting position tucked under your rib cage. Moreover, the vagus nerve travels through your diaphragm alongside your esophagus. The movement of your diaphragm expanding and contracting with your breath helps create a gentle massage and natural stimulation of your vagus nerve. Ideally, the intercostal muscles that sit between your ribs are also able to expand and contract with your breath. They open out to the sides

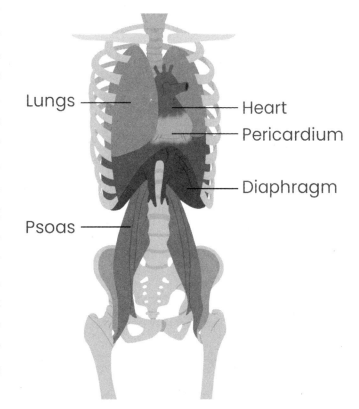

Lungs —

Heart

Pericardium

Diaphragm

Psoas —

and contract to midline. These movements create more space for the expansion and contraction of your lungs.

The Psoas-Diaphragm Connection

The connective tissue of your diaphragm is also deeply connected to your psoas muscles. The psoas muscles are located on the sides of your lower abdomen, and they attach to your lower spine, as well as to your inner leg, just below your pelvis. The psoas muscles are key players in the fight-or-flight responses of the sympathetic nervous system. They work with other hip flexor muscles and contract to draw your legs into your core, helping you protect your visceral organs. The contraction of these hip flexors also helps you prepare to run away from danger or kick in self-protection. Chronic and unresolved trauma can be held as tension in these muscles.

The psoas muscles are part of a complex grouping of muscles and fascia at the base of your pelvis that comprise the pelvic floor. The pelvic floor acts as a secondary diaphragm that helps form the foundation for the breath. In addition, the pelvic floor provides support for your abdominal organs. When you have a history of trauma, you can sometimes carry excessive tension in the pelvic floor, which tends to restrict the breath. Because the connective tissues extend throughout your body, tension in the pelvic floor is often linked to tension in your neck, throat, and the soft palate at the back of your throat. The soft palate functions as an additional, third diaphragm in the body, and it too is meant to move with the breath. Once again, it is common to carry tension in the muscles of the neck and throat when you have a history of trauma, and most people carry some degree of tension in these areas.

The good news is that conscious breathing helps you release chronic patterns of tension held in the connective tissue that links all of these areas of your body. Simply deepening your breath already creates change, and adding gentle movements that mirror your breath can amplify the benefits of mindful breathing. Before moving into the breathing practices, reflect on these key areas of your body that are involved with the breath. If you find these questions are challenging for you, know that you can return to them when you feel ready.

As you reflect on the anatomy of the breath as described above, I invite you to notice any patterns of tension that you may hold in your throat, chest, diaphragm, belly, psoas muscles, or pelvic floor. Take some time to write about these experiences in your body and how this may be connected to any past stress or trauma. Remember, you do not need to go into detail about the traumatic events. You are simply acknowledging the past to finding the healing that is available for you here and now.

_____

_____

_____

_____

_____

_____

Take some time to identify anything that has already helped you safely release some of the tension that you feel in your body. Do you have a movement practice (e.g., yoga, stretching, working out, dance, etc.) that has helped you find a sense of greater freedom or empowerment in your body? Have you ever received massage or bodywork that has helped release physical tension? Have you participated in any somatic or body-centered psychotherapy practices that have resulted in greater ease or release in your body? What were your experiences of these practices? Were they positive, neutral, or negative?

_____

_____

_____

_____

_____

EXERCISE
Using Breath to Sense the Body

If you feel ready, you can explore the following body awareness and conscious breathing practices. You might choose to start with just one of these and devote three to five minutes of your day to conscious breathing.

You can listen to the audio track of this guided practice available at http://www.newharbinger.com/54162.

Diaphragmatic Breathing

1. Begin to bring your attention to your breath. Notice the rhythm of your breath as it enters and leaves your body. Take your time here.

2. When you would like, begin to add in conscious movement of your diaphragm with your breath. It can be helpful to place your hands just below your ribcage, so they cover your diaphragm and you can feel its movements.

3. Begin to consciously expand your abdomen as your diaphragm moves downward on your inhale. Allow everything to relax as your diaphragm lifts back into place during your exhale. Notice the expansion of your ribcage on your inhalation, which creates a gentle stretch and opening of the sides of your body. As you exhale, let everything soften.

As you continue to move your diaphragm with your breath, see if you notice any changes in the sensations in other areas of your body. For example, you might notice a subtle opening in your chest or a broader one in your belly.

Sensing the Chest, Neck, and Throat

1. While engaging in diaphragmatic breathing, bring your attention upward to your chest, neck, and throat. Place one hand over your chest and your other hand on the back of your neck.

2. Notice any movements in these areas of your body, including:

3. Movements in your **chest** because of the expansion and contraction of your lungs,

4. Subtle movements around your **shoulders**,

If you notice tension in your **upper back, shoulders, or neck,** try squeezing your shoulders upward toward your ears before letting them relax downward.

Exploring the Mouth, Tongue, and Jaw

1. Soften your jaw by slowly opening and closing your mouth until you rest your lower teeth away from your upper teeth.

2. Trace the top of your mouth with your tongue, by starting behind your teeth and moving the tip of your tongue across the hard palate until you find the soft palate at the roof of your mouth.

3. Yawn to release tension from your throat, mouth, and tongue.

4. Relax your tongue and soften your jaw again.

5. Continue to notice any sensations in your chest, shoulders, throat, and jaw as you sense your breath moving in and out.

Sensing Your Lower Belly and Pelvic Floor as You Breathe

1. As you continue to breathe diaphragmatically, see if you feel comfortable bringing your attention to the three-dimensional bowl of your pelvis.

2. **Place your hands over your lower abdomen**, below your navel.

3. While you do not have lungs in your pelvis, **imagine breathing into this area** of your body.

4. **Notice any subtle movements** of expansion or contraction within your lower abdomen and pelvic floor in response to your breath.

5. Even if you do not notice any sensations or movement here, it is a powerful practice to send your intention to breathe into your lower belly and pelvic floor.

Take some time to write about your experience of these breathing practices. Were there any areas of your body that felt open and receptive to your breath? Were there any areas where you experienced tension or restriction? What emotions arose for you as you explored these practices? What support do you need to continue to explore your relationship to your breath?

_____

_____

_____

_____

_____

_____

_____

_____

The Vagal Brake and Heart Rate Variability

A key element of the polyvagal theory is a concept known as the *vagal brake*. The idea is that the sympathetic nervous system functions like a metaphorical gas pedal and the vagus nerve serves as a metaphorical brake pedal. When the *vagal brake* is engaged, it reduces the sympathetic nervous system's influence and slows down your heart rate. When you remove the vagal brake, your heart rate will speed up again.

Let's take a look at the relationship between your breath, vagus nerve, blood pressure, and heart rate. The vagal brake is located within the sinoatrial node of the heart, also known as your heart's built-in pacemaker. Imagine a river flowing through a wide expanse. This river tends to move slowly. However, now imagine this river tightening as it begins to flow through a narrow canyon. Naturally, the current increases as the volume of water travels through a smaller channel. When you inhale, your diaphragm typically expands, which increases the amount of space for your lungs and heart. Like the wide expanse for our river, there is plenty of space for your blood to travel through the heart, and your blood pressure and heart rate naturally slow down.

Your vagus nerve is particularly sensitive to blood pressure sensors called *baroreceptors* that are located within the sinoatrial node of your heart. When the vagus nerve senses this reduced blood pressure and heart rate, it carries a signal up to your brainstem to speed the heart rate back up. This is necessary because it will allow your heart to pump blood upward to your brain, so that you don't get lightheaded. In response, the vagal brake lifts and your heart rate increases. When you exhale, your diaphragm draws in and upward, which reduces that amount of space for your heart and lungs. Now the space for the heart narrows, and just like a river flowing through a canyon, your blood pressure and heart rate will increase. This time, your vagus nerve carries the baroreceptor signal up to your brainstem, which initiates a slowing down of your heart as the vagal brake reengages. This entire process facilitates *homeostasis* and healthy *vagal tone*, which are defined as an optimal balance between your sympathetic and parasympathetic systems.

When we breathe in a rhythmic and paced manner, we cultivate smooth and rhythmic transitions between the sympathetic and parasympathetic nervous systems. This process is referred to as coherence (McCraty and Zayas 2014). Coherence facilitates a relaxed and attentive state. You are not so relaxed that you are going to sleep, which would be a dominant parasympathetic state, nor are you climbing a mountain, which would be a primarily sympathetic state. Coherence is a flexible nervous system that helps us handle the inevitable challenges of life, because we are able to transition relatively smoothly between sympathetic and parasympathetic states. For example, if you feel activated by something a family member says, you might notice a temporary spike of your sympathetic system, but you have the capacity to recover and return to a sense of calm and ease. Moreover, when you are in coherence, you are better able to make decisions, handle conflicts, and navigate difficult moments, because you notice that you feel triggered or activated and—rather than reacting—you remember to take a mindful pause.

Having a history of trauma can disrupt coherence, making it more common and more painful to feel stuck in a distressing nervous system state. This, like all repercussions of trauma, is a symptom that benefits from self-compassion rather than self-judgment. Keep in mind that some individuals who are neurodivergent also find it challenging to switch between nervous system states. For example, it might be difficult to transition to bed after being highly focused on a task, or conversely, to get up after relaxing on the couch when it is time to leave the house. While a coherent state has benefits for mental, emotional, and physical well-being, it is also important to honor and respect the diversity of nervous systems in human beings.

Coherence is associated with an increase in vagal tone, which is measurable using tools that track *heart rate variability*. Heart rate variability (HRV) is determined by comparing the number of heartbeats on the inhalation to the number of heartbeats on the exhalation. Once again, in a high heart rate variability pattern, you will have more heartbeats on the inhalation and fewer on the exhalation. Moreover, you will start to observe a rhythmic pattern of heartbeats in relationship to the breath. A low heart rate variability pattern is more disjointed or unpredictable. It is associated with reduced emotional regulation and poor attentional capacity. Whereas a high heart rate variability pattern is associated with reductions in anxiety, depression, and PTSD symptoms. It helps you have a greater capacity to handle stress and to recover from difficult moments. You can think of this as the physiological basis for resilience.

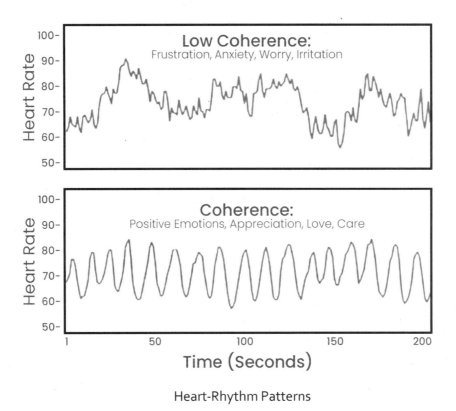

Heart-Rhythm Patterns

The best way to increase vagal tone, heart rate variability, and coherence is to simply breathe in a rhythmic and paced manner. I invite you to take a pause for another conscious breathing practice. This *paced breathing* practice, also known as *resonant frequency breathing*, invites you to breathe rhythmically, so that your inhalations and exhalations are approximately the same length, to enhance your vagal tone (Pagaduan et al. 2019).

EXERCISE
Paced Breathing

- For this breathing practice, find a five-second inhale and a five-second exhale. As you breathe, silently count. In time and with practice, you will develop a felt sense for your paced breathing, and you can let go of actively counting. You can also adjust the timing to support your comfort. While it is ideal to breathe in and out through your nose, you can breathe through your mouth if needed. Try starting with two minutes of paced breathing at a time. Once you feel comfortable with the practice, you can increase to five minutes per breathing session.

- Write down anything that you notice in response to this breath practice. Pay attention to any emotions that arise or subtle shifts you feel in your body. What did you notice during the breathing practice? How about after you were finished? There is no right or wrong response to any practice. Noticing what arises for you helps you understand yourself and adapt your breathing practices in the future.

_____

_____

_____

_____

_____

A Grateful Heart

While breath alone is an excellent way to enhance your mind-body health, you can also amplify the benefits by combining mindful breathing with a gratitude practice. Focusing your mind on anything that evokes a natural sense of appreciation not only helps boost your mood, but also is also linked to improved sleep quality, immune system health, and a greater sense of optimism about the future (Emmons and McCullough 2004). Because of the important link between our emotions and our autonomic nervous system, gratitude is another way to initiate an upward spiral of positive emotions. Gratitude helps boost parasympathetic activity, which brings balance to the stress of daily living.

Gratitude practices, such as writing down a list of things that you are grateful for, are also associated with increases in heart rate variability and coherence. Moreover, the combined effects of conscious breathing and gratitude amplify the emotional and physical health benefits of both (McCraty and Zayas 2014). Consider trying the following heart-focused breathing practice for yourself. Importantly, as you explore gratitude, it is vital to be gentle with yourself and the process. You cannot force a feeling of gratefulness on yourself; however, you can create an invitation to reflect on positive experiences in your life, and in doing so, you might start to feel a natural sense of appreciation and warmth arise within you.

EXERCISE
Practice Gratitude

1. Find a comfortable position to engage in a conscious breathing practice for the next three minutes. If you would like, set a timer.

2. Bring your attention to your heart and imagine your breath flowing in and out of it. Slow down your breathing and allow your breath to move a little deeper as you continue to breathe, while focusing your attention on your heart center. You might return to the five-second inhalation and exhalation, but do not concern yourself with counting if it's distracting.

3. Bring to mind anything that evokes a natural feeling of appreciation, warmth, or gratitude. You might imagine a loved one, pet, or place that evokes feelings of ease,

peacefulness, or calm. Continue breathing in this manner, gently focusing your mental awareness on gratitude while you sense your breath moving in and out of your heart.

4. Once you feel finished, let go of the focused breath and simply notice what you feel in your body and mind. Take several minutes to engage in a follow-up gratitude practice: Write down as many things as you can think of that you feel grateful for in this moment.

_____

_____

_____

_____

_____

_____

_____

_____

Remember that you can return to this practice as often as you would like and that the greatest benefits tend to occur with repeated practice.

Conscious Breathing for Body-Mind Health

In chapter 1, we discussed how trauma can lead us to have overactive sympathetic states that are associated with hypervigilance, anxiety, excessive worry, or panic. You can think of this as a state of *hyperarousal*. In contrast, when the parasympathetic nervous system is dominant, you are more likely to be in *hypoarousal*, or underarousal, in which you feel fatigued, low energy, powerless, hopeless, or depressed. It is profoundly empowering to know that you can come back to a place of balance or ease.

Balance isn't a static state of being. Rather, it involves small adjustments that help you adapt to the ongoing demands of life. Imagine riding a bicycle. In order to balance and move freely, you are constantly making adjustments to the speed of your feet on the pedals and the orientation of your body on the seat. In regard to your nervous system, balance involves knowing when and how to downregulate your nervous system out of hyperarousal and how to upregulate and reenergize your nervous system when you are in hypoarousal.

The breathing practices in this section aim to place you in the driver's seat of your nervous system. Typically, when you emphasize your inhale, you activate your sympathetic nervous system by briefly removing the vagal brake, upregulating your nervous system and giving you energy (Telles et al. 2011). Conversely, breaths that emphasize the exhale have a calming effect, because you are engaging the vagal brake and thus the parasympathetic nervous system, allowing you to slow down and rest (Laborde et al. 2021). One way to emphasize the parasympathetic effects of the breath is to add humming, which accentuates your exhale. Humming amplifies the nourishing benefits of conscious breathing by stimulating of your vocal cords and inner ear (Porges and Lewis 2010). Adding brief retentions of your breath has also been linked to improved heart rate variability (Russell et al. 2017). Therefore, two common variations of breath retention are offered here: the box breathing technique and the 4-7-8 breath. Also included is the well-researched cyclic sighing breath, which seems to immediately calm the nervous system and foster a felt sense of relief (Balban et al. 2023).

Most importantly, I invite you to explore the effects of each of the following breath practices. You may discover that what is offered as a calming breath practice feels energizing to you, or the reverse. Use these practices as opportunities to study your relationship to your breath and identify what helps you create a greater sense of balance in your own nervous system. You can practice at any time by downloading this list from http://www.newharbinger.com/54162. Take some time after each practice to write down your observations.

Energizing breath: To explore this enlivening breath, take a long inhalation as you bring your arms up over your head, and then let out a short exhalation as you lower your arms to your sides. Typically, you only need to find two or three of these breaths to notice a rapid increase in alertness.

Cyclic sighing breath: Create a two-part inhalation in which you inhale part way, to half of your lung capacity, and then without pause continue into a second inhale to fill your lungs. Now, find an extended exhalation. You might choose to create an audible sound to your sigh such as an "ahh." Continue three to five rounds of this breath.

Extended exhale breath: Begin to inhale for a count of four and exhale for a count of eight. You can also adapt the counting to find a breath that is more comfortable for you, such as an inhale for a count of two and an exhale of four. It is often beneficial to engage in this practice for at least three to five minutes. If you would like, set a timer to support this practice.

_____

_____

_____

_____

_____

Humming breath: As with the extended exhale breath, enjoy a long, slow release of your breath, and add in humming. You might choose to find a single tone, hum a favorite song, or offer a soothing lullaby to yourself. You might also place one or both of your hands over your heart as you breathe and connect with yourself in a loving manner.

_____

_____

_____

_____

_____

Box breathing: Inhale for a count of four, pause at the top of the inhalation for four, slowly release your exhalation for four, and then rest for four. Remember, you can vary and adjust these numbers to find a breath pattern that best serves you. Explore five to ten rounds of this breath.

_____

_____

_____

_____

_____

4-7-8 breathing: The 4-7-8 breath involves inhaling for a count of four, pausing at the top of the inhalation for seven, and then slowly exhaling for eight. Once again, you can vary and adjust these numbers to find a breath pattern that best serves you. Explore five to ten rounds of this breath.

_____

_____

_____

_____

_____

We do not release the impact of traumatic events all at once, and this is especially true when we've experienced ongoing traumatic events that may have occurred over many years. Your breath is deeply interconnected with your willingness to engage in life wholeheartedly. It takes great courage to choose to breathe deeply. Each breath is an affirmation of your commitment to yourself and your healing journey. You can and will create meaningful change, one breath at a time.

CHAPTER 5

Find the Courage to Change with Bilateral Movements

It is your birthright to feel whole, at peace, grounded, and connected to your deepest self. However, traumatic events can leave you feeling broken or disconnected. This is because traumatic events overwhelm your capacity to cope with the threats that you have faced. In order to survive, you disconnect from painful emotions and bodily sensations. Your brain plays a key role in this process. When you feel disconnected from yourself, it is often because the thinking, feeling, sensing, and action-oriented parts of your brain are not able to effectively communicate with one another (Lanius, Paulsen, and Corrigan 2014). As a result, these areas of your brain begin to function independently of each other. For example, there may be times when your thinking brain is overactivated, leading you to feel "stuck in your head," emotionally cut off, and numb. Other times, your sensing brain might be reacting to the look on someone's face, a loud noise, or a particular smell, which can lead you to feel emotionally flooded; however, if your thinking brain is not online, you might not understand your reaction. When these kinds of experiences happen on a regular basis, they can lead you to feel fragmented, confused, or disjointed.

Scientific research has studied the impact of trauma on the brain extensively. One area that is particularly vulnerable to traumatic stress is the *corpus callosum*, which sits in between the left and right hemispheres of your brain. Memories, sensations, and emotions connected to traumatic events tend to be held within the right side of your brain (Schore 2019). The left side of your brain is specialized for language and gives you a greater ability to focus on the resources that are available to you here and now. When the left and right sides of your brain do not communicate effectively, you might notice a tendency to tell a story about what happened to you with no emotions at all, or feel as if you are reliving the past but cannot put your experience into words. Importantly, your brain has plasticity and can change (Pagani et al. 2012). While it takes time and often therapeutic support, you can build connections and enhance communications throughout your brain. Doing so allows you to reclaim a sense of wholeness and a deep connection to yourself.

This chapter provides the science behind brain integration and explains why rhythmic movements and bilateral stimulation are effective tools for healing. You will be guided through practices that, when used on a regular basis, will support your journey of trauma recovery. These practices aim to help you regulate your nervous system, improve your resilience, and feel more at home in your body.

Trauma and the Divided Brain

When the brain is able to communicate between the left and right hemispheres, you are better able to recognize your emotions and communicate them to others (Schore 2019). Integration between the two sides of your brain helps you pay attention to the big picture of your life while also being able to focus on what is right in front of you (McGhilcrist 2009). Put simply, when the two sides of your brain are working together, you feel integrated and whole. You are able to identify what is important and engage in meaningful actions that provide you with a sense of purpose.

However, the corpus callosum, the area of the brain that facilitates communications between the left and right hemispheres of your brain, is particularly vulnerable to traumatic stress (Jackowski et al. 2008; Rinne-Albers et al. 2016). It has been described as a metaphorical fault line in the brain, which separates in response to the earthquakes of traumatic events (Fisher 2017). This is especially true when trauma happens during childhood, because this critical area is still growing through adolescence (Tanaka-Arakawa et al. 2015).

One of the ways we facilitate healing from trauma is through bilateral stimulation, which enhances communication between left and right sides of the brain. More specifically, Eye Movement Desensitization and Reprocessing (EMDR) therapy invites you to move your eyes bilaterally—meaning on "both sides"—from left to right to help reduce the distress associated with traumatic events. These rapid eye movements mimic REM sleep, which is the stage of sleep associated not only with dreaming but also with helping your brain process all memories, including difficult ones (Stickgold 2002). In addition to the use of eye movements, EMDR therapy also includes other forms of bilateral stimulation, such tapping your hands, rocking from side to side, or listening to alternating sounds through headphones. Engaging in bilateral activity may help improve information processing throughout the brain (Bergmann 2012).

Rhythmic movements between left and right sides of the body create a felt sense of body-mind integration. Moving or tapping the left side of your body corresponds to the right hemisphere of your brain, whereas moving or tapping the right side of your body activates the left hemisphere. Therefore, when you create complex movements, such as crossing the midline of your body by alternately bringing each arm to the opposite leg, you are alternatingly stimulating the two sides of your brain. These cross-lateral movements seem supportive of psychological tasks such as recognizing our emotions and talking about feelings, as well as cognitive tasks like reading and writing (Hannaford 1995).

When healing from trauma, it is beneficial to engage in *psychosensory* practices (Ruden 2005). This means that we integrate psychological resources—such as identifying a positive belief or visualizing a peaceful place—while adding in sensory experiences such as self-applied touch, yoga, therapeutic tapping, or bilateral movements. The following three practices provide you with an opportunity to experience the benefits of these interventions for yourself.

EXERCISE
Alternate Nostril Breathing

First is the yogic practice of alternate nostril breathing, as a tool to support the integration of left and right hemispheres of your brain. Modern research has studied the effects of breathing through alternating nostrils, which helps create balance in the autonomic nervous system (Mondal 2024; Telles et al. 2017). Breathing through your right nostril is associated with greater sympathetic activation, whereas breathing through your left nostril is associated with greater parasympathetic tone (Niazi et al. 2022). When you breathe in a manner that alternates between the two nostrils, you are bilaterally stimulating your brain.

1. Use the thumb of your right hand to close off your right nostril as you inhale through your left nostril.

2. Switch the position of your right hand, using your fingers to close of your left nostril as you exhale through the right. Now, inhale through the right and exhale through the left side.

3. Continue to breathe as you alternate nostrils. You will always move the placement of your hand at the top of the inhale.

4. As you breathe in, visualize a stream of light moving through your nostril, into your brain. As you exhale, that stream of light travels out through the opposite side. Inhaling and exhaling light, filling your brain with light. Continue to breathe as you visualize the light moving through the center of your brain.

5. When your timer goes off, exhale through the left nostril, release your right hand, and for the next two or three breath cycles, continue the same visualization. Picture the light from one side of your brain crossing the center, then exhaling out the other side.

6. Continue this practice for as long as you would like. When you feel complete, let the visualization go, and let go of the focus on your breath. Notice any sensations throughout your body.

7. Take some time to write about your experience of the alternate nostril breathing.

_____

_____

_____

_____

_____

EXERCISE

The Butterfly Hug with Peaceful Place Imagery:

This exercise is the butterfly hug—a resource development technique that comes out of EMDR therapy (Parnell 2008). The brain doesn't differentiate between real or imagined experiences; therefore, visualization is a powerful healing tool that can awaken neural circuitry throughout your brain while helping you sense a deep feeling of relaxation throughout your body. If at any point you find that the bilateral tapping creates feelings of distress, simply stop the movement and reorient yourself to the cues of safety in your surroundings.

1. Bring to mind an image of a peaceful place that helps you feel calm and serene. This place might be a place that you have been or one that you simply imagine. Pay attention to the details of your peaceful place. Are you indoors or outside? What do you see, hear, and feel when in this space? Let this be a sanctuary for your body and mind—a place that allows you to be quiet and reflective. Are you alone or with others? If you invite others into your sacred space, be sure that they feel nurturing and protective.

2. Once you have a strong positive feeling, cross your arms across the center of your chest, in a butterfly hug, so that your hands land in front of the opposite shoulder.

3. Alternately tap left and right hands slowly, about ten times to fifteen times, and then pause to check in with yourself. If the feeling remains positive, you are welcome to tap for longer.

4. Find a pace for your tapping that feels natural and supportive. Let yourself be nourished by any positive feelings that arise in the process. Remember, you can stop at any time if you feel uncomfortable or lose that peaceful feeling.

5. Continue for three to five rounds of tapping, so long as it feels good.

6. Take some time to write about your experience. Know that you can return to this practice as often as you like.

_____

_____

_____

_____

_____

_____

_____

EXERCISE
Tapping for Trauma Recovery

The third practice guides you through a series of tapping points used in Emotional Freedom Technique, or EFT (Craig 2011). EFT guides you to tap on specific acupressure points that correspond to those identified in traditional Chinese medicine, while repeating statements that help you heal your past (König et al. 2019). EFT tapping helps improve connectivity within the brain and creates improved heart rate variability, improved vagal tone, and reduced inflammation (Bach et al. 2019). This tapping practice begins with a statement that helps you set your intention while you tap on the side of your hand. This is followed with statements to support your growth as you sequentially tap on eight points of your body, all listed in the exercise.

You can keep a list of tapping points with you by downloading this image from http://www. newharbinger.com/54162. At the same link, you can also explore the following guided practice by listening to the available audio track.

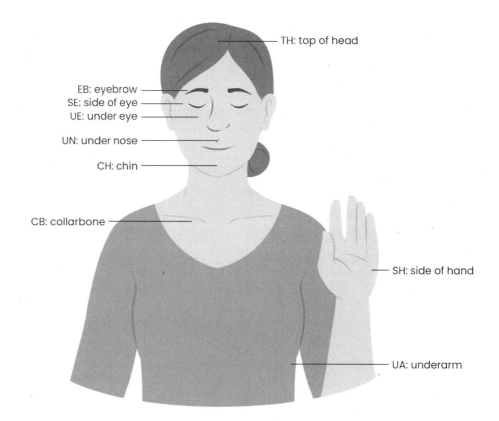

1. Start by taking a deep breath in and out. Take a moment to identify any distress that you are feeling. On a scale from 0 to 10, what is the intensity of your distress, with 10 being the worst amount of discomfort and 0 being no distress at all?

2. When you feel ready, begin tapping with the fingertips of one hand on the outside (pinky side) edge of the opposite hand. Say these words in your mind or out loud, *Even though I have been struggling, I am open to finding more comfort and ease.*

3. Repeat the same action, tapping on the side of your hand, *Even though I have been afraid, I am willing to connect more deeply with myself in this moment.*

4. One more time, on the side of your hand, *Even though part of me is hesitant, I celebrate my courage in engaging in this practice.*

5. As you proceed to the face, choose whether you would like to tap on just one side of your face or on both sides simultaneously. If you work with just one side, you will stay on that side for the first three tapping points. Begin tapping on the inside of your eyebrow(s) as you say to yourself, *I am willing to be present with my thoughts and feelings today.*

6. Move to the side of your eye, *It is okay if I have difficult thoughts and feelings, they are all part of me.*

7. Under the eye, *My thoughts and feelings are welcome here, I do not need to fight them.*

8. Under the nose, *I am simply aware of my thoughts and feelings, and I am courageously showing up for myself today.*

9. Under the mouth, *I am learning to compassionately acknowledge my thoughts and feelings, and to let them go.*

10. Under both of your collarbones, *I am choosing to be gentle with myself throughout my healing journey.*

11. Under the arm that corresponds with the eye you started with (if you did both sides, tap under one arm and then the other), *I know that healing takes time and I am willing to be patient with myself and the process.*

12. Top of the head, *I am reclaiming a deep sense of connection to myself step by step.*

13. As you finish this first round of tapping, take a moment to tune back in to the intensity of your distress. How strong is it now on the 0 to 10 scale? Has the number changed?

14. If you notice residual distress, which is common, return to the tapping for another round, as you continue to focus on the intention of creating more space for your thoughts and feelings. When you feel complete, take some time to write about your experience.

_____

_____

_____

_____

_____

_____

_____

_____

_____

_____

_____

Brain and Body Integration

Up until now, we have discussed the benefits of increasing communication between the left and right hemispheres of your brain, across the corpus callosum. It is also beneficial to optimize the connection between the upper and lower areas of your brain. Doing so provides you with a felt sense of brain and body integration. Within the brain, the process of building these connections requires that the prefrontal lobes of your brain communicate with a specialized region called the insula, which is located deep within the cerebral cortex. The insula is the part of the brain that receives input about your bodily sensations, and the prefrontal cortex allows you to consciously reflect on your experiences (Damasio 1999). Another region of the brain central to body awareness is the cerebellum, which is part of the brainstem, at the base of the brain. The cerebellum is associated with movement, coordination, and balance, and it helps you process your emotions.

Two additional key centers found within the brainstem are the medulla and pons, which work with the vagus nerve to regulate your body's vital autonomic nervous system functions, such as breath rate, heart rate, sleep-wake cycles, temperature, and visual orientation. When you engage your prefrontal cortex to observe your bodily experiences, you are being mindful of signals of dysregulation of your autonomic nervous system, and you can more easily adjust how you are breathing or moving to take care of yourself. Moreover, when these upper and lower areas of the brain are communicating well, you are able to integrate sensations, feelings, and thoughts, so that you can make meaning about your life experiences. Together, these help you feel an overall sense of self.

As discussed, when you have experienced a traumatic event, it is common for your sensory processing sensory system to feel heightened or diminished. At times, you might feel hypersensitive to noise, bright lights, touch, or smells. Other times, you might feel disconnected from the external sensory reality, perhaps as if the world around you is surreal or very distant. Having an integrated sensory system allows you to feel where your body begins and ends in space, and helps you experience yourself as whole, grounded, and centered.

One of the ways that you can enhance sensory integration and build communication between your brain and body is to explore movements that engage the primitive reflexes. Reflexes are preprogrammed movements that are hardwired between the brain stem, spinal cord, and muscular systems. For example, these primitive movements allow you to turn your head toward or contract your body away from a frightening sound. They also support you in reaching with curiosity toward novel experiences when you feel safe. When we have experiences of stress and trauma, our reflex responses can become activated, repetitive, or stuck. More specifically, several early reflexes can get activated by trauma. Two of them are the fear paralysis reflex and the Moro reflex, which work together to facilitate our startle response—our limbs expand away from center with a sharp inhale, followed by a contraction to center. When unresolved, these reflexes can exacerbate symptoms of anxiety, insomnia, fatigue, lack of trust, depression, vulnerability to emotional overwhelm, freezing, dissociation from one's body, and vulnerability to asthma or digestive issues.

A third key reflex that can interfere with your well-being is the orienting response, which in response to trauma can lead you to feel frozen when there is a loud sound or bright light. Like a deer in the headlights, your body tenses, and you feel vigilantly aware of your external environment. Ideally, your orienting response supports the curiosity and exploration that helps you gather knowledge about the world around you. This orienting response will be naturally awakened when you're exposed to anything new or unexpected. If your orienting system assesses that your environment is neutral or pleasant, you are more likely to feel motivated to move toward and explore the space and people around you (Blanchard and Comfort 2020). Conversely, when you assess that your environment is threatening, a defensive orienting response will lead you to withdraw, constrict your energy, or engage the cascade of autonomic stress responses (Berger 2019).

When a defensive reflex response is activated, it is beneficial to engage in exercises that provide your brain with proprioceptive feedback. Proprioception helps you sense where your body begins and ends in space. This sensory system utilizes feedback from your vestibular system, which is located in your inner ear and within the joints of your body. Vestibular and proprioceptive feedback work with the sensory processing systems in your brain to reduce over- or under-stimulation. Vestibular practices typically involve rocking, swaying, bouncing, and balancing movements, which open up the channels of communication between your joints, inner ear, and brainstem. That communication, in turn, helps your nervous system register your body's relationship to gravity. You can complement these practices with proprioceptive input through self-applied touch, pushing, and body weight activities that help you feel more grounded—which, in turn, helps you feel safe.

The following self-applied touch and movement practices provide your brain with proprioceptive and vestibular sensory inputs, enhance brain and body integration, and help you come out of the automatic defensive activation of your primitive reflexes. Reflex integration is supported through rocking, bouncing, swaying, and movements that cross the midline of your body.

Most importantly, you do not need to wait for something to be wrong in order to engage with these practices. In fact, it is more beneficial to engage in these practices on a daily basis. Doing so helps build your resilience to stress by enhancing your capacity to recover quickly into states of ease. You might choose to engage in all of these movements sequentially in a single practice; however, the rocking movements can sometimes evoke vulnerable emotions. If that is the case for you, please know that this is a normal part of developing nervous system resilience. These emotions are coming to the surface as part of your healing process. If this occurs, pace yourself and honor your process by recognizing this as a cue to pause and attend to yourself with compassion, or seek a coregulating person to lovingly offer their presence. Return to these movements as you feel ready.

- **Hold your head:** Place one hand on the base of your skull, over your brainstem, which is where the alarm bells of your brain come from. Place your second hand over the front of your forehead and imagine enhancing your reflective, calming, and creative problem-solving capacities. With your hands holding your head, send your breath between your two hands to enhance integration between the front and back of your brain.

- **Hold your feet and lower legs:** Gently hold or massage the bottom of your feet. Place both your hands over the sole of one of your feet, holding the arch, and massage each of your toes. You can also wrap your hands around your ankle, massage around and above your heel, and move upward to massage your calf. Repeat on the other foot and leg.

- **Rhythmic rocking:** Rocking movements involve moving your body forward and backward. Find a gentle rocking movement while seated in a chair. As you roll your pelvis back, allow your spine to lengthen. Next, roll your pelvis forward and let your spine curl forward. Continue to move back and forth rhythmically between these two shapes, inhaling as you lengthen your spine and exhaling as your curl it. After about ten rounds, take a pause and receive yourself as you are. You can also use a swing or rocking chair.

- **Swaying movements:** Sway from side to side while seated. The important element of these movements is to cross the midline of your body. Let yourself sway to the right and left as you continue to breathe. If you would like, you might also reach an arm over your head, then across to the opposite side of your body. You can imagine that you are reaching to pick a piece of fruit of the tree. Alternate hands, continuing to reach with one hand and then the other. After about ten rounds of swaying movements, return to center and pause.

- **Bouncing:** To find bouncing movements, I suggest standing with softly bent knees. Begin to rhythmically bounce on and down as you soften through your face, jaw, shoulders, arms, and hands. You might even let your voice go along with the bouncing as you sigh and allow any sound to come out. You can also explore bouncing movements while standing on a mini-trampoline or sitting on a physio ball. When engaging in bouncing practices, notice what happens as you deepen your breath and how this might support you to let go of any resistance to the movement.

- **Balancing:** Another way to stimulate your vestibular system is to explore a balancing practice. Start with a simple exercise by lifting one foot off the floor. Try removing your shoes for this practice, as the muscles in your foot will be better able to support you through micromovements. If balancing is a challenge for you, you can begin with support, placing one hand on a chair or the wall. With or without that support, gently bring one of your feet off the floor. You might keep the toes of your raised foot touching the ground or you may bring your entire foot off the floor by resting it on top of your other foot. You might also place your foot on the inside of your standing leg, like a yoga tree pose. Stay in this shape for about five to seven breaths. Once you feel comfortable with the basic balancing practice, you can challenge yourself further by closing your eyes while balancing. Another way to challenge yourself is standing on a balance board, which has a flat top with a round underside, creating an unstable surface to stand on. Remember to find the right amount of challenge—a level that is supportive of your growth and does not overwhelm you.

- **Pushing and pressing:** It is beneficial to engage in pushing and pressing movements, which will stimulate your proprioceptive system, helping you feel grounded and secure. Stand close to a wall and press your hands into it. As you do so, keep a soft bend in your knees, and press your feet into the floor. Begin to sense your body in between the pressing actions of your hands and feet. Return to seated and press your hands downward, with firm pressure, onto the tops of your legs. Then, using that same firm pressure, begin to massage the backs of your calves on your lower legs, moving downward toward your heels.

- **Integration:** Find a position, seated or lying on your back, to rest and support the integration of these practices. You might enjoy using a weighted blanket to help you settle into stillness. When you feel complete, take some time to write about your experience on the lines below.

_____

_____

_____

_____

_____

_____

_____

_____

The Windows of the Soul

The eyes have often been referred to as the windows of the soul. When you feel safe, your eyes tend to sparkle and express warmth. This is because your eyes are deeply connected to your social engagement system, which is a function of the upper circuits of your vagus nerve. Your eyes allow you to receive the people around you and help you communicate to others how you are feeling. While you might try to hide your true emotions by controlling the muscles of your face, it's far more difficult to stop your eyes from revealing how you really feel. When you feel connected and excited to see someone, your eyebrows tend to lift, making your eyes appear brighter and more welcoming. In contrast, when you are tired, your eyelids grow heavy. Or, when you are stressed, you might furrow your brow, which contracts the muscles around your eyes, making them appear smaller. Moreover, when under an extreme threat, your pupils dilate, which lets in more light and helps you scan your environment. Therefore, individuals who have experienced traumatic events at night are often able to describe the scene as if it happened in broad daylight.

These physiological responses to threat are essential for our survival; however, when traumatic activation remains unresolved, we often continue to carry strain in the muscles around our eyes. The muscles around the eyes have connections at the front and back of the skull; therefore, eye strain can lead to headaches and neck tension. Moreover, many of us spend a lot of time on computer and phone screens, which strains our eyes and takes a toll on our nervous system. Recovery from any kind of eye strain invites to you to release unnecessary tension patterns, so that you find a sense of resolution and return to a feeling of ease in your body. One way to release eye tension is to rest your eyes by gazing at a far-off horizon to counteract the tension of looking at a screen. Moving your eyes to a faraway focal point also appears to be beneficial for the tone of your vagus nerve (Bowan 2008). You can try this for yourself.

EXERCISE
Soften Your Gaze

It is helpful to engage in this practice while outdoors or in a location where you can look out a window. Find a point for your gaze that is on the far horizon or softly gaze at something in the distance. Let your gaze rest there for at least twenty to thirty seconds, as you soften the muscles around your eyes. You might notice that it is also helpful to release any tension that you are holding in your jaw, mouth, and tongue, as these facial muscles tend to be connected to tension around your eyes. Continue to breathe with this soft gaze for long as you would like.

Bilateral Eye Movements and the Neurochemistry of Courage

Our eyes naturally move from side to side as we walk through the world. It's a way of observing our environment. From an evolutionary perspective, this action is necessary for survival. It allows us to scan the world for food and potential predators. These lateral eye movements suppress the brain's fear response while simultaneously signaling the release of dopamine, a neurotransmitter that helps increase a felt sense of courage, pleasure, and reward (Balban et al. 2021).

As discussed, bilateral eye movements are a key component of trauma recovery in EMDR therapy. These eye movements appear to reduce the activation of a key structure in your brain called the *amygdala*, which is highly involved in your fight-or-flight response, by letting your upper brain regulate better (Kaye 2008). Simply put, these eye movements help make traumatic memories less intense. Eye movements can also enhance positive states, helping you find a greater sense of stability and resource within yourself (Korn and Leeds 2002).

Within EMDR therapy, we cultivate a specific state of attention called *dual awareness*—your ability to attend to small amounts of tolerable distress while remaining oriented to your felt sense of safety and connection. In general, it is not recommended to work on your most disturbing traumatic memories without the support of someone trained to work with post-traumatic stress reactions. This is especially true when attending to relational losses and traumatic events where you felt neglected or abandoned. Those kinds of wounds benefit greatly from being with another person who offers their care and compassionate presence, because you want to be able to work through your symptoms without reliving your traumatic past. However, when you attend to smaller, tolerable amounts of distress while attending to cues of safety, you can build your capacity to be with vulnerable emotions. Doing so prepares you for the deeper work of trauma recovery. Learning to turn toward painful emotions or memories while remaining connected to your resources strengthens a coherent sense of self. Earlier, you learned about the term coherence and how this nervous system state, which is marked by high heart rate variability, is associated with emotion regulation and a greater capacity to reflect on your stress response without reacting. Likewise, coherence as discussed by Daniel Siegel (2010) refers to your capacity to reflect on the whole range of your human experiences—the pain, the hurts, and your wounds, alongside the beauty of this world, your strengths, and your capacity for hope.

EXERCISE

Bilateral Eye Movements with a Pairing Practice

The final practice of this chapter offers bilateral eye movements as a tool for self-care to reduce the distress associated with everyday challenges and stressors, such as feeling stuck in traffic or having a difficult interaction with a friend.

1. **Find cues of safety and connection:** Begin noticing any cues that let you know that you are currently in a space that is safe enough. Do you feel connected to your breath and body? Is there any additional support that you need to access a sense of safety and connection? Is there a word or color that matches this sense of safety, connection, or resource? If so, write the words or put the color in the circle below labeled Resource. So long as you continue to feel safe and connected to yourself, begin to move your eyes slowly from left to right to strengthen this positive feeling. Your eyes can be open or closed. Continue moving your eyes back and forth for about ten rounds of movement. On completion, pause and notice what you are aware of in your body and mind.

2. **Courageously connect to an area of distress:** Is this a good time for you to attend to an area of distress in a loving manner? Can you access a sense of self-compassion? If so, identify one area of distress that you would like to work with today. As you reflect on it, notice what you feel in your body. What emotions are present for you? Are there any strong beliefs or thoughts that arise for you as you reflect on this area of distress? Is there a word or color that matches this feeling of distress? If so, write or draw the color in the circle below. Once again, move your eyes back and forth for ten rounds of bilateral movements. Your eyes can be open or closed. On completion, pause and notice what you are aware of in your body and mind.

3. **Pendulation of your attention:** Look at the two circles below that represent your resource and your area of distress. Once again, bring your attention to your experience of safety and connection, and add the bilateral eye movements. Next, bring your attention back to your area of distress and add the bilateral eye movements. You can imagine a pendulum swinging back and forth, between the resource and

the distress. Take your time with this process and continue for as many rounds as feels supportive to you.

4. **Enhancing coherence:** Finally, take a moment to notice how you feel as you notice your connection to resource and your area of distress at the same time. What arises within you as you hold these two experiences together? What arises in your body? What emotions or thoughts arise now? Take your time to write about your experience on the lines below.

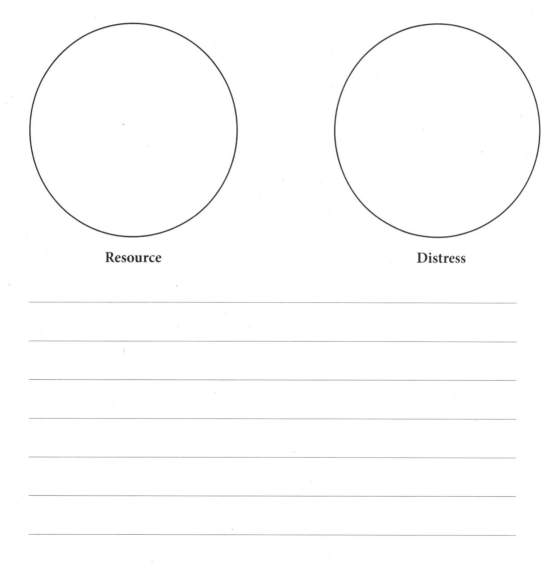

Resource   **Distress**

_____

_____

_____

_____

_____

_____

You are so much more than the difficulties, wounds, or traumatic events of your life. You are whole, wise, and worthy of care. Your willingness to engage in the practices in this workbook is a testament to your strength and courage.

CHAPTER 6

Mindful Movement to Bolster Your Nervous System

In the immediacy of a shocking or traumatic event, it is common to feel shaky, panicky, and overwhelmed. Ideally, these events are short lived, and when they are over, we can return to a sense of safety in which our body releases the impact of the fearful event. However, when these stressful events are repeated and ongoing, we do not have an opportunity to release the stress from our bodies. Over time, remaining in high-arousal states of threat and anxiety can exhaust our resources, which wears down our capacity to cope with daily stressors. When our resources are depleted, we begin to feel fatigued, depressed, and a desire to withdraw from the world. You might say to yourself, "I cannot handle any more pain." Therefore, it is essential that we include body awareness and, when possible, movement as part of the healing process.

From the perspective of the polyvagal theory, we typically move through the "tiered response to threat" that you learned about in chapter 1. As a review, we initially attempt to resolve a threat via the social engagement system. Here, we reestablish a sense of safety by calling for help or reaching out for people that are sources of connection and compassion. If we are unable to find protection or resolution of the threat, we then utilize our sympathetic nervous system's fight-or-flight response. Once again, if we cannot get away from or resolve the threat, our last resort is to engage the evolutionarily older parasympathetic response of the dorsal vagal circuit. This leads to feelings of helplessness, hopelessness, and somatic experiences of lethargy, fatigue, fogginess, or dizziness. All of these responses are driven by the innate intelligence of your nervous system—they are all aiming to help you to survive.

While these responses to the world may have once been necessary, remaining in them for extended periods of time can become problematic. You might feel stuck in ongoing feelings of panic, hypervigilance, or anxiety. Conversely, you might feel stuck in fatigue or collapse. In the classic fable "The Tortoise and the Hare" these two creatures are in a race. The hare runs so fast he exhausts himself, whereas the tortoise, who moves slow and steady, wins the race. If you are constantly running, unable to stop and rest, you will end up wearing yourself down. In contrast, if as a tortoise, you were stuck in your shell, you might not know how to get yourself moving again. The goal of the movement invitations in this chapter are to get you up and moving, so that you can make it to the finish line and feel great along the way.

Initially, it might feel frightening to move your body, especially if you have felt shut down. Disconnecting from your body or dissociating from your feelings was an important way of protecting yourself from intolerable emotions such as fear, sadness, or shame. It is beneficial to progress slowly when engaging in body awareness and movement. If you push yourself to connect to your feelings and sensations too quickly, you might trigger an impulse to shut down again—like a rubber band that has been stretched, you snap back into contraction and self-protection. Once again, a slow and steady approach to reawakening your body through gentle movements allows you to befriend your body at a pace that supports your growth.

Building on the previous chapters, this chapter deepens our discussion of the science of movement and why mindful mobilization is a key to trauma recovery. You will learn more about key concepts of polyvagal theory, including the vagal brake and vagal efficiency. You will explore for yourself tools to not only reclaim your mental health, but also recover from the physical health consequences of trauma. You will then have an opportunity to engage in practices that help you climb up the polyvagal ladder, as you safely release unnecessary tension from your body.

Embodiment and Trauma Recovery

Moving your body helps climb the *polyvagal ladder* in a manner that reverses the tiered response to threat (Dana 2018). Climbing the ladder out of defensive survival states allows you to access the resilience of your social engagement system, which enhances your personal well-being, as well as your relationships with others. For example, you climb the ladder out of a shutdown or collapsed state by reawakening your body through gentle movements, such as wiggling your fingers and toes. This can help you sense your body in the here and now. As you feel ready, you begin to mindfully engage full-body movements that awaken your sympathetic nervous system, while simultaneously recognizing that you are safe enough here and now. Doing so helps you experience yourself as strong and empowered now. You learn to reclaim a felt sense of your own aliveness.

The sympathetic nervous system initiates movement because of a rapid release of neurochemicals that increase your heart rate and release energy to the muscles of your body. In the context of a threat, this process prepares you to fight or flee from a dangerous situation. In the context of safety, your sympathetic nervous system allows you to play and feel joy.

When you have a history of trauma, you may only associate the bodily sensations of sympathetic activation with memories of times when you were in danger and expectations of a negative outcome. For example, you might automatically begin to think something is wrong when you feel a rapid heart rate, quickened breath, or sweat on your skin. Peter Levine, the developer of a body-centered approach to trauma recovery called somatic experiencing, refers to this process as over-coupling, in which a nervous system state is only associated with negative consequences (Levine 2010). When you uncouple your sympathetic nervous system from fear and threat-based associations, you are able to reclaim your capacity to feel excited, empowered, energized, or exuberant. This allows you to dance, practice yoga, go to the gym, or climb a mountain.

Your sympathetic system can be thought of as mobilization, and your parasympathetic nervous system brings you into immobilization or stillness. You reclaim your relationship to excitatory states through mindful mobilization. Moreover, when you have felt paralyzed by a parasympathetic immobilization response, it is often necessary to remobilize your body to climb the polyvagal ladder out of a shutdown response.

From the perspective of somatic psychology, sympathetic mobilization sends energy to your extremities. You tense your arms and legs, preparing to run away or protect yourself. You might also feel an urge to reach your arms out for connection or call out for help. When we are unable to complete these actions, our minds and body do not experience resolution. Our instinctual movements have been thwarted or blocked (Levine 2010). Deep within us, we long for a sense of completion. We are seeking a sense of closure so that our brains can finally register that the traumatic event is over.

In order to find resolution, you learn to attend to the sensations of your body and explore what movements would help provide a sense of completion. For example, you might notice a knot in your throat and begin to explore making sounds that help release emotions that are contributing to the tension you feel. Likewise, tension patterns in the jaw, chest, shoulders, belly, and hips can all carry remnants of incomplete actions. Your body can help guide your healing process, allowing you to sense how you want to move to unwind and release the burdens of the past.

Within somatic experiencing, we approach the healing processing using a tool of *titration* (Levine 2010). Titration is a scientific term that refers to the combining of two chemicals such as an acid and a base. For example, if you take a large amount of vinegar and baking soda and mix them together, you can generate an explosive reaction. However, if you place a few drops of vinegar into a spoonful of baking soda, the chemicals will bubble up and settle back down. Likewise, if you turn your attention toward all of your emotions and sensations at once, you are likely to feel overwhelmed. A titrated approach to healing invites you to engage with your body by briefly bringing your attention to your sensations while doing small movement experiments.

You take breaks as needed to notice what arises and integrate each experience into your overall sense of self.

Embodiment refers to the process of bringing conscious awareness to your bodily sensations. If you have felt disconnected or numb, it can take time to develop a sense of comfort in your body. A titrated approach lets you slowly attend to sensations, one area of your body at a time. You might start with noticing your fingertips, hands, toes, feet, or the top of your head, as these areas might feel less emotionally vulnerable. Eventually, you can explore noticing your throat, chest, belly, and hips, which tend to carry more tension that might feel connected to traumatic events from the past. Before we progress into the guided movement practices, take a moment to explore your own relationship to your body.

Do you have a sense of how traumatic events may be held as tension patterns in your body?

_____

_____

_____

_____

_____

What support do you need to help you focus on the sensations of your body without becoming overwhelmed?

_____

_____

_____

_____

_____

The Vagal Brake and Enhancing Vagal Efficiency

An essential concept within the polyvagal theory is the metaphorical *vagal brake*. If your body were a car, you can think of the sympathetic nervous system as a gas pedal and your parasympathetic system as the brakes. Since your vagus nerve is always associated with the parasympathetic system, it too functions like a brake, reducing your heart rate and respiratory rate as your slow down or come to a stop.

The vagal brake is located in the sinoatrial node of your heart; this is also known as your heart's pacemaker. The ventral vagal, sympathetic, and dorsal vagal systems all have neural inputs located in this area of your heart. Once again, the sympathetic input accelerates the heart. In order for this to happen, the vagal brake, which ordinarily slows down the heart, must lift. The ventral and dorsal vagal inputs slow down your heart; however, they do so in two different ways. The ventral vagal brake slows the heart down gradually and smoothly and can easily lift again, which allows you to respond flexibly to the normal demands of life. In contrast, the dorsal vagal circuit functions as an abrupt brake that leads to a rapid reduction of heart rate, which imitates the feigned death or faint response.

Ideally, the ventral vagal brake helps us meet the physiological demands of our lives. Even simple tasks such as moving from lying down to standing require an increase in your heart rate, so that you get enough oxygenated blood to your brain. If the vagal brake did not lift, you would feel dizzy, lightheaded, or in some cases experience a vasovagal syncope, which leads to fainting. Conversely, while we need the vagal brake to lift to help us mobilize, we also need it to reapply so that our heart rate does not stay elevated or continue to increase. If the vagal brake did not reapply, you would feel chest pain, a racing heart, and begin sweating profusely.

Vagal efficiency refers to how quickly the vagus nerve helps you adapt everyday stressors (Porges 2017). When vagal efficiency is low, we tend to notice a low tolerance for exercise and reduced capacity to handle stress. Moreover, when your nervous system is out of balance, it can have consequences for your health. Remaining in high sympathetic tone for extended periods can lead to weight gain, blood sugar imbalances, an increased susceptibility to heart disease, and suppressed immunity. Conversely, remaining in a parasympathetic shutdown can lead to inflammation, joint pain, digestive distress such as irritable bowel syndrome, and an increased vulnerability to autoimmune conditions (Scaer 2014). Vagal efficiency can be compromised by ongoing early developmental trauma, and can be an underlying cause of post-viral conditions such as long-COVID syndrome (Kolacz et al. 2020; Woo et al. 2023). Reduced vagal efficiency leads to the dysregulation of the autonomic nervous system, also known as dysautonomia. Since your autonomic nervous system is linked to your digestive, cardiovascular, endocrine, and immune systems, it is not uncommon for imbalances to show up as physical health concerns. This checklist can assist you to reflect on the following symptoms and how they might show up for you.

Symptoms of a Dysregulated Autonomic Nervous System:

- Sleep disturbances

- Fatigue

- Brain fog

- Reduced tolerance for exercise

- Postural orthostatic tachycardia syndrome (POTS)

- Chronic fatigue syndrome

- Fibromyalgia

- Inflammation and chronic pain

- Autoimmune conditions

- Irritable bowel syndrome (IBS) and other gut-related conditions

- Long-COVID syndrome

- Eczema, hives, and acne

It is important to be gentle with yourself if you relate to any of the items on this checklist. Having compassion for your symptoms provides a foundation for healing. Moreover, the tools you are learning throughout this entire book help build vagal efficiency. In addition to the natural vagus nerve stimulation, conscious breathing, and reflex integration strategies you learned in previous chapters, this chapter offers an additional set of tools through mindful movement. Using the skill of titration, you can build greater tolerance for movement and exercise. You do so by mindfully engaging in incremental challenges, such as exercise routines that temporarily activate your sympathetic nervous system followed by phases of rest that allow you to recover through the reengagement of the vagal brake. The practices within this chapter will help you build greater capacity to mobilize your body without exhausting your resources.

Stand Your Ground

One of the key components of a body-centered approach to healing is grounding. Grounding refers to sensing the connection between your body and earth. When we have a history of trauma, we tend to pull away from gravity as a way to disconnect from the pain of our emotions or somatic sensations. The exercises for the previous chapter that focused on enhancing vestibular and proprioceptive sensory awareness assist with grounding. In addition, movements that awaken sensations in your legs help you feel rooted and help your brain sense that you are supported by the earth beneath you. The following guided practice for grounding will help you explore this process for yourself.

EXERCISE
Grounding

Grounding exercises are often a good way to begin any somatic practice, as they will help you feel safe enough to let go of emotional and physical tension.

1. Find a standing position with your feet set just wider than your hips, so that you can feel your legs supporting you. Gently bend to your knees so the joints of your legs are not locked or braced. Begin to shift your weight from side to side, so that you can sense the weight of your body in your legs. Take some time to sense and feel your feet on the ground beneath you.

2. Imagine that you have roots that extend downward through your hips, legs, and feet into the dark, rich soil. Stay with this image for several breaths as you exhale into the ground beneath you.

3. Amplify your experience by finding a safe outdoor space where you can place your bare feet on the earth. Whether you are standing on a patch of grass in your yard, a sandy beach, or in a pine forest, take your time to notice your natural environment. Wiggle your toes and move your feet by pressing them into the earth. Notice the temperature and textures of the earth below you.

4. Whether practicing indoors or outside, take some time to notice what you feel in your body now. Write about your experience on the lines below.

_____

_____

_____

_____

_____

Mindful Mobilization

Mindful mobilization invites you to pay attention to the sensations in your body while engaging in slow and consciously chosen movements. The goal of these movements is to support you in coming out of chronic patterns of fight, flight, freeze, or faint. For example, you might shake or wiggle through your arms and legs to come out of a freeze. Or you might push through your arms to sense yourself as powerful and capable of protecting yourself. As discussed earlier, we grow throughout our entire lives, and positive neuroplasticity refers to shaping your growth in a wanted direction. Exercise is one of the most powerful ways to jump-start neuroplasticity because it stimulates the release of many feel-good chemicals, such as dopamine, oxytocin, and GABA, while increasing blood flow to your brain (El-Sayes et al. 2019). There is an enhanced window of plasticity

immediately following movement that can allow for positive change. When you combine movement with mindfulness, you can simultaneously enhance your mental fitness.

The next set of practices invites you to reflect on your relationship to your body and movement, followed by invitations to explore mindful mobilization. Before diving into any somatic practice, orient to the cues that let you know that you are safe in the here and now, or practice the grounding exercise as a preparatory step. While engaging in mindful movements, focus on strengthening thinking patterns and beliefs that help you to recognize that you are powerful, free to move, capable of protecting yourself, and safe to express yourself now. You can say the suggested phrases out loud or in your mind. You can also adapt these phrases to meet your unique needs. Generally, it is beneficial to repeat each of the exercises about three to five times to give yourself a chance to fully embody the experience. You may notice that your heart rate or breathing accelerates in response to some of the exercises.

EXERCISE
Mindful Mobilization

You can explore this guided practice by listening to the audio track available at http://www .newharbinger.com/54162.

1. Wiggle your fingers and toes as you say to yourself, *I am free to move my body now.*

2. Slowly push your arms forward as if pressing a large rock or boulder off your chest. You can also push against a wall. Notice how it feels for you to begin with bent elbows and slowly lengthen out through your arms. With either action, say to yourself, *I am powerful and capable of protecting myself now.*

3. Take slow, mindful stepping movements with your feet, as if you are slowly walking in place, while saying to yourself, *I can walk away from anything that hurts me.*

4. Take in a deep breath and let out an audible sigh, roar like a lion, or find any other sounds that feels satisfying to you. You might also explore saying words like "no," "stop," or "stay away," as you use your voice to assert your boundaries. Accompany this release with the words, *My voice is loud and clear!*

5. Pick up a pillow and give it a tight squeeze with your hands and arms. Let this pillow represent anything that you are holding onto from the past that is no longer needed or that is not of benefit for your future. Hold on tight for about ten seconds and then let go. As the pillow falls out of your hands, say to yourself, *I am letting go and releasing anything that no longer serves me.*

6. Once again place a pillow in front of you. This time, let the pillow represent your future. Visualize yourself as strong, capable, empowered, compassionate, and kind to yourself. Extend your arms and hands out in front of you, and take hold of this version of you. Grasp the pillow with your hands and bring it into the very core of your being. Let yourself feel the power of your reach. Once you have the pillow close to your chest, allow yourself to embody this vision of yourself. Stand up tall, letting your face and body express your worthiness and dignity, as you say to yourself, *I know who I am!*

7. When you feel complete with these practices, take some time to notice what you feel in your body. Did your heart elevate? How did your breath respond? Were you able to sense a settling in your nervous system following the movement? Use the lines below to explore your process.

_____

_____

_____

_____

_____

_____

Playful Pandiculation

In chapter 4, you learned about fascia, which consists of connective tissues that work with the vagus nerve to facilitate communications between your brain and your body. Mindful movement plays a key role in helping your brain sense what is happening in your body. The vagus nerve senses subtle changes in the fascia that arise when you stretch or contract the muscles of your body. When we observe animals, they naturally engage in movements that function like a full-body yawn. Perhaps you can imagine the way a cat or dog moves when they are waking up from a nap. Known as pandicular movements, these are free-form movements that alternate between stretching and contracting motions. These movements help release the buildup of chronic muscular tension (Hanna 2004).

EXERCISE
Pandiculation

Rather than following a prescribed set of movements, this next practice invites you to listen to the sensations of your body while following any intuitive or instinctual movement impulses.

1. You can explore this practice from seated, standing, kneeling on your hands and knees, or laying down. This is also a lovely practice to engage in first thing in the morning, before climbing out of bed.

2. Begin by sensing how you feel in your body. Notice any areas of tension or ease.

3. Find a contraction of your body, so you get smaller and tighter, like a ball of yarn. Take one or two breaths in this shape, then reach and expand away from your center in any way that feels natural to you. Imagine that you are just waking up in the morning as you yawn yourself awake.

4. Now, find a variation of these movements by contracting one side of your body while the other side expands.

5. Take several breaths as you continue to alternate between the contracted and expansive shapes with your free-form movements. Imagine that you are your favorite animal, stretching and waking up from a nap.

6. When you feel complete, take your time to sense and notice how you feel in your body now. Write about your experience on the lines below.

_____

_____

_____

_____

_____

Shake It Out

It is quite common for tension, emotions, and energy to become blocked in your body. Imagine that the energy and emotions moving through your body are like a river. Ideally, the water in your river flows freely. This helps you feel clearheaded, relaxed yet energized, and capable of handling whatever comes your way. However, there may be times when you feel too much energy or too many feelings moving through you. In that case, your river might look more like a flash flood. On days like that, the grounding exercise from earlier in this chapter can help you feel rooted and supported. Other times, you might sense that your energy is lethargic or unavailable to help you meet the needs of your day. Using our metaphor of the river, you might notice that the water is caught in eddies or there simply isn't enough flow.

While trauma might be a root cause of these energetic states, it is not always necessary to understand why you feel sluggish or drained. Animals in the wild do not stop and think about their narrow escape from danger. Instead, they come out of a freeze response simply by shaking and remobilizing the body. Likewise, sometimes simply engaging in a short burst of vigorous movement is enough to get you back into the flow of your life. Doing just five jumping jacks or putting on your favorite song and dancing in your living room helps release the blocks that are holding you back. These bursts of movement can also help you "get out of your head" as you bypass your thinking brain and get into your body. Once again, these vigorous movements help build vagal efficiency; however, you want to progress at a pace that feels supportive to your growth. If you notice a post-exercise malaise or fatigue, this is simply a sign to progress slowly as you build your tolerance. You might begin with a chair-supported movement practice or exercise for very short time periods.

The following practices offer suggestions for how you might bring more vigorous movement into your life. Remember to listen to your body for feedback about the pace that is right for you. Pause after each practice and let your heart rate and breath settle back down.

EXERCISE
Shake It Out

1. From either a standing or seated position, shake out your arms and legs vigorously. Let the movement come into your hips, torso, and shoulders. Continue for thirty seconds and then pause. Notice what you feel in your body now. If you feel good, you can repeat this practice and lengthen the time you spend shaking.

2. Play an upbeat song that will support you to dance and shake your body. My personal favorites are "Shake It Off" by Taylor Swift, "Shake It Out" by Florence and the Machine, and "Human" by The Killers. Imagine that you have just come out of the pool, and shake the water off your body. Or, imagine that you are shaking off any of the difficult things you've been through. You can let it go!

3. Challenge yourself to do five to ten jumping jacks or run in place for thirty seconds. Notice the elevation of your heartbeat. Can you receive the sensations in your body as signs of your aliveness?

4. Go outside for a vigorous walk or jog. If this feels new or intolerable for you, begin with just two minutes of fast walking and build from there. Notice how your stamina for vigorous movements grows day by day.

5. When you feel complete, take some time to notice what you feel in your body now. Did your heart rate elevate? How did your breath respond? Were you able to sense a settling in your nervous system following the movement? Use the lines below to explore your process.

_____

_____

_____

_____

_____

You can continue to add on longer practice times, as you build your endurance and tolerance for exercise. This might involve finding a gym where you feel empowered, or exercise classes and yoga instructors in your community or online who support your growth.

Defying Despair

Sometimes it may feel as if nothing you do is going to make a difference. You might feel despair or a sense of hopelessness for your future. If none of the movements helped you release the energy stuck in your body, then you might need to give voice to your experience just as it is. You might say, "nothing helps," or acknowledge the stuckness you feel by saying, "I'm stuck," out loud. When we acknowledge the truth of how we feel, it is common for something new to emerge.

Sometimes the feeling of despair and hopelessness is connected to times from the past when nothing you did was going to make a difference. If there was no way to be heard, get your needs for connection met, or protect yourself in an unsafe situation, it is common to internalize a felt sense of powerlessness. The key to change is recognizing that now can be different. There are always small changes that you can make that will make a difference in the outcome of the hour, your day, and your week. Each small action you take to build your resilience accumulates and ultimately helps you feel empowered to create a meaningful and fulfilling life.

Giving voice to a part of yourself is a form of movement—it might be more subtle than the whole-body movements that you have explored thus far, but it is no less powerful. As you embrace mindful mobilization, notice how it feels to reawaken your life-force energy!

CHAPTER 7

Rest and Restore Through Trauma-Informed Mindfulness and Relaxation Practices

At the end of any journey, there is a period of rest. This is an important phase of trauma recovery, as it allows your body heal while your mind integrates new insights or perspectives that you have gained along the way. The practices that support restful states are relatively simple; however, when you have a history of trauma, becoming still might feel uncomfortable. Rather than feeling peaceful, you might notice that your mind begins to race when you sit to meditate or that you feel anxious as bedtime approaches. The anchoring resources of applied polyvagal theory can help you reclaim your ability to soften into the quiet spaces.

Research suggests that mindfulness practices have many benefits to your overall well-being. They have been shown to reduce inflammatory biomarkers, reduce stress, and reduce heart disease while improving symptoms of chronic pain, anxiety, depression, and PTSD (Trakroo and Bhavanani 2016). Drawing on the resources you discovered in the previous chapters, this final chapter invites you to reflect on your relationship to rest. You will explore the physiology of restful states from a polyvagal perspective, followed by the healing power of trauma-informed mindfulness and relaxation practices.

The Physiology of Rest

Your parasympathetic system can be thought of as your immobilization system. In the context of safety, immobilization allows you to rest in stillness, meditate peacefully, and sleep well at night. Softening into stillness supports your immune, digestive, cardiovascular, and endocrine systems. Each time you engage in a restorative practice, you have an opportunity to downregulate your defensive physiology, which promotes states of calmness.

As you have learned, polyvagal theory teaches that when you are in danger, this immobilizing system can bring you into a freeze response, in which you are on high alert while motionless, or a faint response, in which you are in hypoarousal and collapse. Both the sympathetic and parasympathetic nervous systems can become over-coupled with a threat response. When your parasympathetic nervous system is over-coupled, you might notice that you feel on guard when you try to relax. Or, you might notice feelings of fear or panic arise when you try to go to sleep at night. This might occur if you had to brace to protect yourself or feign sleep to avoid being harmed. Or, you might feel chronically tense without fully knowing why, leaving you feeling amped up rather than relaxed. Finally, you might notice that when you engage in relaxation techniques, you end up feeling groggy and disoriented rather than rested.

You can cultivate a new relationship to rest using the skills of polyvagal theory. To do so, focus on awakening your ventral vagal "social engagement" system. For example, prior to moving into any mindfulness or relaxation practice, you can revisit the practice you learned in chapter 1 that invited you to look around your space and orient to the cues that let you know that you are safe now. Since relaxing your body involves softening your defenses and coming out of fight or flight, you might feel afraid that you will not be able to protect yourself. Therefore, the practice of mindful resting invites you to remember that you have choices throughout the practice. You can choose whether you would like to have your eyes open or closed, and you can choose to move your body at any time or end the practice if you feel uncomfortable. These kinds of choices help your nervous system recognize that you are not trapped or required to engage in any practice if it does not feel right. Moreover, David Trealeaven, author of *Trauma-Sensitive Mindfulness*, suggests choosing a word or short phrase that helps to focus your mind on positive or loving attention (Treleaven 2018). When your mind wanders, use your word or phrase to focus your attention. Knowing that traumatic events can disrupt your ability to sleep or relax, I invite you to compassionately reflect on your relationship to rest with the following questions.

What is your relationship to rest and relaxation? Is it challenging for you to fall or stay asleep at night? How have you felt when meditating or doing a guided relaxation practice? How might your relationship to restful states be connected to traumatic events from your past?

_____

_____

_____

_____

_____

_____

Mindfulness

Sometimes we inaccurately believe that mindfulness is synonymous with maintaining a meditation practice. While beneficial, meditation is not for everyone. Mindfulness, on the other hand, is better understood as the act of paying attention and has a much broader application. I invite you to view mindfulness as a kind and respectful way to relate to yourself and the world around you. It is a practice rooted in self-acceptance and builds your capacity to honestly reflect on your own humanness. Moreover, mindfulness helps you build your capacity to stay present even when you feel uncomfortable. Ultimately, you can practice mindfulness anywhere—while doing the dishes, driving your car, and especially when interacting with others. That said, there are benefits to giving yourself structure to practice being mindful in a controlled environment. Mindfulness meditation provides you with this opportunity.

Within a mindfulness meditation, you give yourself a set amount of time to focus on *being here now*. Of course, this is easier said than done. It is not always easy to slow down when our minds and bodies are attuned to a fast-paced world. You might prefer to start with the mindful walking meditation provided below, as it gives your mind a focal point in the predictable movement of your feet. Another option is to explore the guided mindful cup of tea exercise, which invites you into the sensory experience of the moment. If you feel that a seated mindfulness practice is right for you, the final practice in this section will help you find a focal point for your mind to anchor your attention. In trauma-sensitive mindfulness, a mental anchor is like securing a boat in the safety of a harbor, so that it is less exposed to the winds and waves of the open seas (Treleaven 2018). In this meditation, you give your mind a focus, so that you are not feeling flooded by distracting or disturbing thoughts. You can explore mindfulness with any or all of the next three practices.

EXERCISE
Mindful Walking

When engaging in this mindful walking practice for the first time, begin with a short experiment of about three to five minutes. If you would like, you can set a timer. You can choose to practice indoors or outside. You can wear shoes or be barefoot.

1. Find a comfortable position while standing still, with a slight bend in your knees so that they are not locked.

2. Take a moment to connect to your breath and the sensations in your body.

3. Slowly begin to walk while focusing on the sensations in your legs and feet. Coordinate your breath with your movement. Inhale as you lift your foot off the ground and exhale as you set your foot back on the earth.

4. Notice the sensations of your feet rising and falling with each step. Notice the shifting weight in your hips and legs.

5. If you become distracted, slow down or pause until you can sense your feet and legs once again. Return to the mindful movement when you feel ready.

6. When you feel complete, pause in stillness and reflect on your experience of this practice.

EXERCISE
A Mindful Cup of Tea

This practice involves mindfully sipping a cup of tea.

1. Begin to boil water for your tea.

2. As the water heats up, choose your favorite tea and a teacup that has the right feeling for you. Notice the weight of the empty cup in your hands.

3. When the water is ready, pour the water into your cup to steep your tea. Feel the warmth of the steam or the sides of the cup. Is there a scent to your tea? If so, receive this sensory experience.

4. Once your tea has cooled, mindfully take your first sip, sensing the hot water and flavor of your tea in your mouth.

5. Continue to slowly, mindfully sip your tea. Notice how it feels to simply be here, now, with this experience.

EXERCISE
Mindfulness Meditation

To begin this mindfulness meditation practice, look around your space and orient your attention to any sensory details that let you know it is safe for you here and now. Find a place where you can sit comfortably. Take your time to adjust your space by adding pillows so that your back feels supported. If you are just beginning mindfulness mediation, it is beneficial to start with three to five minutes. Set a timer if you would like. As you gain comfort with this practice, you might increase your practice time to ten to twenty minutes. You can use following phrase to support this practice.

1. As you breathe in, mentally say the words *I am*, and as you breathe out, mentally say to yourself *here now*.

2. Continue breathing with this intention, *I am here now*, as you practice. Your eyes can be open or closed.

3. It is natural for your mind to wander. This is a natural part of the practice. You can simply bring your attention back to this short phrase, *I am here now*, whenever it feels right and supportive to you.

4. To end the practice, open your eyes if they were closed, and reorient yourself to the space around you. Bring movement back to your fingers and toes. Take a few deeper breaths as you prepare to continue with your day.

_____

_____

_____

_____

Rest Well

Many of us push our bodies past our limits by staying busy or using caffeine to stay awake during the day. We may be fearful of slowing down because we do not want to sense our bodies or emotions. Once we begin to slow down, we might sense how exhausted we actually are. Therefore, when we do take the opportunity to rest, instead of relaxing peacefully, we crash. We mindlessly scroll on our phones or binge-watch shows on TV. Instead, we want to learn how to rest well. Perhaps this is especially true if we grew up in a culture that does not have a siesta or midday nap.

Ironically, research suggests that it is our ability to rest that helps us be more efficient, focused, and successful in our work (Pang 2016). One way to rest well is to integrate a nap into your daily routine. However, not all naps are made equal. Naps around sixty to ninety minutes long provide opportunities for the brain to integrate new learning, because you have enough time to drop into slow-wave sleep and REM, which enhances memory consolidation (Mednick and Ehrman 2006). Since PTSD is linked to impairments in memory consolidation, napping can assist your trauma healing process. By napping mindfully, you can take your time to ensure that you are feeling safe and comfortable. If you are going to nap for an hour or more, it is helpful to do so right after lunch, between 1 and 3 p.m. This will prevent you from being too groggy and ensure that your nap doesn't interfere with your sleep at night. Keep in mind that excessive napping is associated with negative outcomes including depression, cognitive decline, and diabetes (Mantua and Spencer 2017). Excessive napping refers to taking multiples naps, naps that are longer than ninety minutes, or intermittent dozing throughout the day. As you can see, resting well requires moderation. For many of us, it is not realistic to take an hour off in the middle of our day. In this case, integrating a power nap into your daily routine is a worthy alternative. A ten-to-twenty-minute rest period can be enough to help you feel alert and refreshed. When engaging in the mindful napping practice below, experiment with different durations and times of day until you find the ideal nap for you.

EXERCISE
Mindful Napping

Set an alarm to wake you up after your chosen nap time to ensure that you do not oversleep. You can also set an intention for your nap time by saying, out loud or quietly to yourself, *I am resting to support my healing journey.* Take your time to get comfortable, whether you are napping on the couch or in your bed. Before closing your eyes, look around your space and orient your attention to any cues that let you know that you are safe here and now.

An alternative to this process is to engage in a relaxation practice in which you remain awake but deeply rested. Relaxation practices have been studied for decades as a tool to consciously engage the body's parasympathetic rest-and-digest response (Benson and Proctor 2011). Likewise, within the yoga tradition, the practice of yoga nidra, or yogic sleep, promotes relaxation by guiding your attention to one area of your body at a time. This helps your brain move away from thinking and planning, and into simply paying attention to sensation. The benefits of guided relaxation include reduced stress and anger; improvements in symptoms of anxiety, depression, and PTSD; lowered blood pressure; reduced inflammation; improved hormonal balance for women; fewer tension headaches; and improvements in memory (Kumari and Karunaratne 2022; Lahl et al. 2008; Pandi-Perumal et al. 2022; Stankovic 2011). The following guided relaxation practice integrates a parasympathetic-dominant breathing pattern, in which your exhalation is longer than your inhalation. The goal is to deeply relax without falling asleep.

EXERCISE
Guided Relaxation

You can explore this guided practice by listening to the audio track available at http://www.newharbinger.com/54162.

1. Look around your space and orient your attention to the cues that let you know that you are safe now. Find a comfortable position, either seated or lying down. While it is beneficial to close your eyes for this practice, if doing so creates any discomfort, it is important to know that you and can always reopen your eyes at any time. Set an intention for your relaxation by saying, out loud or quietly to yourself, *I am resting to support my healing journey.*

2. Take a breath in through your nose for a count of two, then exhale through your mouth with your lips pursed, as if you were sending your breath through a straw, for a count of eight or until your exhale is complete. Repeat this breath two more times as you relax your nervous system. Then, return to breathing normally.

3. Begin to bring awareness to your body as you focus your attention on your feet. Notice any sensations of your feet as they make contact with the ground. Begin to expand your attention as you shine the light of your awareness toward your ankles, shins, and calves.

4. Illuminate the fronts and backs of your thighs by bringing your attention to your upper legs. Pay attention to the entirety of your legs and feet as you return to the breath you practiced earlier. Inhale through your nose and exhale slowly through your pursed lips, letting the air out slowly, as your legs completely relax. Repeat this breath twice more as you soften and relax your lower body.

5. Now bring your attention to your abdomen, and focus on the sensations there. Expand your awareness to include your chest and shoulders.

6. Next, broaden your attention to the back of your body as you sense how your upper and lower back make contact with the chair, sofa, bed, or floor behind you.

7. Sense your entire torso as you return to the breath—as you inhale through your nose for a count of two, then exhale slowly through pursed lips. Exhale completely as your torso softens and releases into gravity. Repeat this breath twice more as you relax your torso.

8. Bring your awareness to your upper arms, lower arms, and hands. Sense the entirety of your arms and hands as you return to the breath by inhaling through your nose and exhaling slowly through your pursed lips. Repeat this breath twice more as you soften and relax your arms.

9. Focus your attention to include your face, the back of your head, and the top of your head. As you breathe normally, relax the muscles of your face. This time, simply breathe in and extend your exhalation without tensing the muscles of your face.

10. Now expand your awareness to include your entire body, from the top of your head to your feet. For just two breaths, allow your awareness to fill your entire body on your inhalation, and to let go of any tension as you exhale slowly. Breathe normally as you rest here for three to five minutes.

11. As you feel ready, begin to wiggle your fingers and toes. As you wake up your body, circle your hands around your wrists, and circle your feet around your ankles. If your eyes were closed, slowly reorient your attention to the world around you as you open your eyes.

12. Before moving on with your day, I invite you to take some time to reflect on this guided relaxation practice by writing about your experience on the lines below.

_____

_____

_____

_____

CONCLUSION

Enhancing the Rhythms of Regulation

As we come to a conclusion, I invite you to reflect on your journey. You have learned the knowledge and skills to support you and the health of your mind and body through the science of applied polyvagal theory. Hopefully, you are already feeling more balanced, stronger, and more capable of turning toward yourself with compassion and kindness. Your growth and gains will continue. Moreover, repeated and consistent engagement with these practices is the key to well-being. Each time you revisit a practice, you nurture positive neuroplasticity. Within this conclusion, you will be guided to develop daily routines out of the skills that you have learned. This will optimize the benefits of this workbook and support your integration of the material. Day by day, you will rewire your nervous system out of trauma reactivity and become the flexible, resilient, and joyful person you are meant to be.

Rhythms of Regulation

Your body has built-in rhythms of regulation that help you sleep well at night and digest your food. For example, your circadian rhythm is a twenty-four-hour cycle that regulates sleep, hormone release, body temperature, hunger cycles, and digestion. Likewise, your resting respiratory rate and heartbeat are rhythms maintained by the medulla deep within your brainstem. As you have likely experienced, traumatic events disrupt these rhythms. The good news is that you can reset these rhythms using the tools you have learned. To do so, it is beneficial to engage in these practices on a daily basis in a relatively predictable manner. This process will help reset your nervous system through the rhythms of regulation.

One of the most important routines to reclaim body-mind health is to have a regular sleep schedule—going to bed and waking up around the same time each day. You can lovingly create a bedtime routine for yourself, just like you would when caring for a young child. Ideally, it is beneficial to go to sleep around 10 p.m. and to wake up around or shortly after sunrise. Doing so helps to reset your circadian rhythm. It is especially beneficial to go outside in the early morning light (Wright et al. 2013). When creating a bedtime routine, it can be helpful to reduce blue light exposure before bed by limiting your use of electronics after dark. You might also take a bath or listen to soothing music before bed as part of your routine. Sometimes it is helpful to use a sound machine to block out noises that might keep you awake. If you do wake up in the night, can you speak to yourself in a loving voice, just like you might settle a child who woke up from a dream.

It is also beneficial to give your digestive system regular rhythms by eating at consistent intervals during the day. This can help manage your blood sugar and reduce the likelihood that unexpected drops in blood pressure could initiate a threat response. Likewise, the sympathetic nervous system can become activated by sugar, caffeine, and other stimulants. In contrast, a balanced diet supports the health of your autonomic nervous system. It can also be beneficial to give yourself time to digest your food before going to sleep at night to reduce the likelihood of having acid reflux, which could disrupt your sleep. Over time, you might notice that your bowel movements begin to occur at regular times as well.

As you have learned, a balanced autonomic nervous system alternates between sympathetic and parasympathetic states flexibly throughout your day. Engaging in regular exercise routines and mindful rest throughout your day helps with this process. Exercise enhances the health of your cardiovascular, respiratory, and muscular systems. Honoring your tolerance for exercise, you will find the right pace that allows you to integrate movement routines into your daily life. Likewise, you have learned about the importance of incorporating regular rhythms of rest and relaxation throughout your day. Once again, it may be important to begin with shorter practices and trauma-informed approaches to relaxation.

Perhaps the most basic rhythm of regulation discussed throughout this workbook is reclaiming your ability to move smoothly and flexibly between sympathetic and parasympathetic states. Natural vagus nerve stimulation, conscious breathing, and reflex integration practices support you to create optimal nervous system flexibility that we call coherence. When you are in a state of coherence, you transition relatively smoothly between sympathetic and parasympathetic, which helps you recover from the everyday stressful life events that are inevitable in life. It is normal to experience those stressful moments as a brief spike in your sympathetic nervous system. Coherence gives you the ability to recover, to reflect on your emotional responses to the world, and to make wise, conscious choices about how to respond. Most of us do not live in rhythmic coherence all of the time; however, it is important to know how to get back there. Creating predictable routines around eating, exercising, resting, and sleeping assists with this process.

Take a moment to reflect on your rhythms of regulation. How do you sleep at night? How is your digestion impacted by stress? What is your relationship to exercise? How do you recover from everyday stressful life events? As much as possible, I encourage you to write about these experiences without judgment. Rather, this self-understanding can help you create meaningful change.

_____

_____

_____

_____

_____

_____

_____

_____

_____

_____

_____

_____

Begin to think about new routines that can support you to have more rhythmic integrity during your day. What would support you to build in greater predictability around your meal-times or bedtime routines? When will you be most successful in integrating exercise into your day? What kind of restful practice would best support you?

_____

_____

_____

_____

_____

_____

_____

_____

_____

_____

_____

Create an ideal day starting from the time you wake up. Even though you might not always be able to stick to this routine, design a daily rhythm that would best support you. Take a look at the example provided, however, keep in mind that what works for one person may not work for you. There is no "one size fits all" daily routine. In the space below, design your own daily routine that feels realistic and manageable within the context of your life.

EXERCISE
Daily Routine to
Regulate the Nervous System

Sample

6:30 a.m.   Wake up

7:00 a.m.   Morning practice (cold-water exposure, self-applied massage, reflex integration practices, journaling, mindfulness meditation, etc.)

7:30 a.m.   Exercise (walking, yoga, weightlifting, hiking, cycling, etc.)

8:30 a.m.   Breakfast

9:00 a.m.   Work (professional activities, parenting, etc.)

12:00 p.m.   Lunch

1:00 p.m.   Nap or guided relaxation

2:00 p.m.   Work (professional activities, parenting, etc.)

5:00 p.m.   Outdoor walk

6:00 p.m.   Dinner

7:00 p.m.   Family or social connection time

9:00 p.m.   Begin winding down for bed (reduced screentime, bath, restorative yoga)

10:00 p.m.   Bedtime

_____   _____

_____   _____

_____   _____

_____   _____

_____   _____

_____   _____

_____   _____

_____   _____

_____   _____

_____   _____

_____   _____

_____   _____

_____   _____

_____   _____

As you continue to grow, I invite you to fine-tune, add to, and amend your daily schedule until you find the rhythms of regulation that work for you.

Final Reflections

Reclaiming your resilience after trauma requires a long-term commitment to yourself and to your healing process. Change doesn't happen all at once. Creating meaningful change in your life is the result of your ongoing commitment to cultivating a felt sense of safety. Remember, every small step counts, and in time, they accumulate. Collectively, your intentions and actions will support your growth and overall well-being. You are equipped with the tools to recognize your nervous system states and counterbalance self-protective defenses with the resources of coregulation, self-compassion, conscious breathing, and vagus nerve stimulation practices. You have learned about the power of bilateral tapping, eye movements, and reflex integration strategies to reset and rewire your nervous system. By uncoupling your nervous system from states of threat, you have learned how to reclaim the joy of movement and the nourishment of stillness. Take some to look back at your responses to the journaling prompts and practices throughout the book. Celebrate how far you have come. Return to these practices on a regular basis until they feel like old friends welcoming you home to yourself.

Keep in mind that when you feel buoyant and supported, you are better able to be a positive influence on others in your life and within your community. This hurting world needs people who are capable of offering kindness, compassion, warmth, and generosity. You are now equipped with the building blocks to not only shape your own life, but also become a source of benefit for others. My deepest wish is that this workbook provides you with the courage and strength to recognize yourself as a source of coregulating goodness in the circle of life.

"For Now We Are Free"

A Polyvagal Poem

There is a pattern hidden in the tapestries of our biology that carries within it a map to our freedom. Like blueprints, there is a pathway to be discovered in the cellular matrix and connective tissues of heart and lungs, belly and brain.

Deep in the very fibers of these precious bodies we inhabit we discover portals to personal and collective liberation.

But this is not where our story begins. No, we must return to a time when we are confined by the binding forces of separation, loss, and heartache. Perhaps a time when you too have felt imprisoned by pain, constrained by your mind, or disoriented by the distress of this broken world.

To a time when you too were locked in this room with no key, no way to escape,
To a time when you too had no choice but to surrender.

Head bowed close to earth,
we are called to descend;
Descend into darkness,
cocooned within,

You settle into the marrow that
carries your existence
Pulsing through your veins
Nothing to do
but to be.

It is here that something new begins to appear;
slowly your eyes adjust,
You begin to sense space and time;
slowly your ears fine-tune themselves to the subtle tones of songs sung in hushed tones passed
down through generations.

And the patterns begin to reveal themselves
They arise
waiting to be discovered,
As if for the very first time.
You find them in this stillness,
Like constellations of light that stand out against the vastness of a blackened sky.
Like a North Star,
A compass in the night.

Perhaps you too have sensed how these moments resonate;
in the pit of your belly,
the catch of your throat,
the ringing in your ears,
The ache in your head,
And the cry called out from the depths of your very own heart,
as if for the very first time, you too are longing to be heard.

Your very own voice,
Your clarion call has been heard

by this benevolent universe that we share,

Love has heard the call

Love has come to guide your way

And you stand, uncertain at this new edge of life.

Oh, but this love is so new, so unfamiliar.

You turn away in fear.

Once and again,

But it is time to let go of what is known for what is yet to be revealed.

And love, she is patient and persists in her quiet manner.

You sense her as the light shifts across the window sill sending a play of shimmers and shadows across this place you have learned to call home.

She returns as birdsong and honeybee,

in the distant ocean roar,

And the howl of the wolf under a NOW full moon.

Suddenly, without realizing it, you too have stepped across the threshold onto the soft green moss, where the ferns unfurl their ancient wisdom inviting you to join them in their dance toward the sun.

It is here that you discover the fibers of connection resonating in your hips as you lay your belly down on the moist earth to embody the primordial movements of salamander and snake.

It is here that you learn to crawl and walk

as if for the very first time.

For these evolutionary blueprints guide you

as they have done for countless other brave souls,

over thousands of years.

Indeed, they are here to guide a path to personal and collective liberation

as we rise up like the tree,

our roots firmly ensconced in the moist, dark earth.

It is here that you look around
as if for the very first time.
You, too, have discovered that you are not alone,
You find soft smiles,
bodies rocking,
drums beating,
dancing storytellers
spinning webs like maps
woven into ritual and song.

Yes, you have arrived.
you are standing on this path,
A trail traversed by countless wisdom seekers who have come before you,
they have left you their guideposts and lanterns to illuminate your way
out of the dark woods.

To the clearing
Where WE arrive.
We join each other,
hand in hand,
heart to heart,
eye to eye,
for now we are free.

References

Al Haddad, H., P. B. Laursen, S. Ahmaidi, and M. Buchheit. 2010. "Influence of Cold Water Face Immersion on Post-Exercise Parasympathetic Reactivation." *European Journal of Applied Physiology* 108: 599–606.

Bach, D., G. Groesbeck, P. Stapleton, R. Sims, K. Blickheuser, and D. Church. 2019. "Clinical EFT (Emotional Freedom Techniques) Improves Multiple Physiological Markers of Health." *Journal of Evidence-Based Integrative Medicine* 24: 2515690X18823691.

Bailey, R., J. Dugard, S. F. Smith, and S. W. Porges. "Appeasement: Replacing Stockholm Syndrome as a Definition of a Survival Strategy." *European Journal of Psychotraumatology* 14: 2161038.

Balban, M. Y., E. Cafaro, L. Saue-Fletcher, M. J. Washington, M. Bijanzadeh, A. M. Lee, E. F. Chang, and A. D. Huberman. 2021. "Human Responses to Visually Evoked Threat." *Current Biology* 31: 601–612.

Balban, M. Y., E. Neri, M. M. Kogon, L. Weed, B. Nouriani, B. Jo, G. Joll, J. M. Zeitzer, D. Spiegel, and A. D. Huberman. 2023. "Brief Structured Respiration Practices Enhance Mood and Reduce Physiological Arousal." *Cell Reports Medicine* 4: 100895.

Benson, H., and W. Proctor. 2011. *Relaxation Revolution: The Science and Genetics of Mind Body Healing.* New York: Simon and Schuster.

Berger, D. 2019. "Primitive Reflexes and Righting Reactions." Dave Berger (blog), May 4. https://daveberger.net/blog/primitive-reflexes-and-righting-reactions.

Bergmann, U. 2012. *Neurobiological Foundations for EMDR Practice.* New York: Springer.

Blanchard, A. R., and W. E. Comfort. 2020. "Keeping in Touch with Mental Health: The Orienting Reflex and Behavioral Outcomes from Calatonia." *Brain Sciences* 10: 182.

Bonaz, B., T. Bazin, and S. Pellissier. 2018. "The Vagus Nerve at the Interface of the Microbiota-Gut-Brain Axis." *Frontiers in Neuroscience* 12: 49.

Bonaz, B., V. Sinniger, and S. Pellissier. 2021. "Therapeutic Potential of Vagus Nerve Stimulation for Inflammatory Bowel Diseases." *Frontiers in Neuroscience* 15: 650971.

Bowan, M. D. 2008. "Treatment of Panic Attack with Vergence Therapy: An Unexpected Visual-Vagus Connection." *Journal of Behavioral Optometry* 19: 155–158.

Cowan, P. A., and C. P. Cowan. 2007. "Attachment Theory: Seven Unresolved Issues and Questions for Future Research." *Research in Human Development* 4: 181–201.

Chen, C., T. K. Tam, S. Sun, Y. Guo, P. Teng, D. Jin, L. Xu, and X. Liu. 2020. "A Multicenter Randomized Controlled Trial of a Modified Valsalva Maneuver for Cardioversion of Supraventricular Tachycardias." *The American Journal of Emergency Medicine* 38: 1077–1081.

Cozolino, L. 2014. *The Neuroscience of Human Relationships: Attachment and the Developing Social Brain.* New York: W. W. Norton.

Craig, G. 2011. *The EFT Manual.* Santa Rosa, CA: Energy Psychology Press.

Damasio, A. 1999. *The Feeling of What Happens: Body and Emotion in the Making of Consciousness.* Orlando, FL: Harcourt.

Dana, D. 2018. *The Polyvagal Theory in Therapy: Engaging the Rhythm of Regulation.* New York: W. W. Norton.

Deppermann, S., H. Storchak, A. J. Fallgatter, and A. C. Ehlis. 2014. "Stress-Induced Neuroplasticity: (Mal)adaptation to Adverse Life Events in Patients with PTSD–A Critical Overview." *Neuroscience* 283: 166–177.

Emmons, R. A., and M. E. McCullough, eds. 2004. *The Psychology of Gratitude.* Oxford: Oxford University Press.

El-Sayes, J., D. Harasym, C. V. Turco, M. B. Locke, and A. J. Nelson. 2019. "Exercise-Induced Neuroplasticity: A Mechanistic Model and Prospects for Promoting Plasticity." *The Neuroscientist* 25: 65–85.

Fazeli, M. S., M. M. Pourrahmat, M. Liu, L. Guan, and J. P. Collet. 2016. "The Effect of Head Massage on the Regulation of the Cardiac Autonomic Nervous System: A Pilot Randomized Crossover Trial." *The Journal of Alternative and Complementary Medicine* 22: 75–80.

Fisher, J. 2017. *Healing the Fragmented Selves of Trauma Survivors: Overcoming Internal Self-Alienation*. New York: Routledge.

Gazerani, P., and B. E. Cairns. 2018. "Dysautonomia in the Pathogenesis of Migraine." *Expert Review of Neurotherapeutics* 18: 153–165.

Goggins, E., S. Mitani, and S. Tanaka. 2022. "Clinical Perspectives on Vagus Nerve Stimulation: Present and Future." *Clinical Science* 136: 695–709.

Gothard, K. M., and A. J. Fuglevand. "The Role of the Amygdala in Processing Social and Affective Touch." *Current Opinion in Behavioral Sciences* 43: 46–53.

Hannaford, C. 1995. *Smart Moves: Why Learning is Not All in Your Head*. Salt Lake City, UT: Great Ocean Publishers.

Hanson, R. 2016. *Hardwiring Happiness: The New Brain Science of Contentment, Calm, and Confidence*. New York: Harmony Books.

Harricharan, S., M. C. McKinnon, and R. A. Lanius. 2021. "How Processing of Sensory Information from the Internal and External Worlds Shape the Perception and Engagement with the World in the Aftermath of Trauma: Implications for PTSD." *Frontiers in Neuroscience* 15: 625490.

Jackowski, A. P., H. Douglas-Palumberi, M. Jackowski, L. Win, R. T. Schultz, L. W. Staib, J. H. Krystal, and J. Kaufman. 2008. "Corpus Callosum in Maltreated Children with Posttraumatic Stress Disorder: A Diffusion Tensor Imaging Study." *Psychiatry Research: Neuroimaging* 162: 256–261.

Kok, B. E., K. A. Coffey, M. A. Cohn, L. I. Catalino, T. Vacharkulksemsuk, S. B. Algoe, M. Brantley, and B. L. Fredrickson. 2013. "How Positive Emotions Build Physical Health: Perceived Positive Social Connections Account for the Upward Spiral Between Positive Emotions and Vagal Tone." *Psychological Science* 24: 1123–1132.

Kok, B. E., and B. L. Fredrickson. 2010. "Upward Spirals of the Heart: Autonomic Flexibility, as Indexed by Vagal Tone, Reciprocally and Prospectively Predicts Positive Emotions and Social Connectedness." *Biological Psychology* 85: 432–436.

Kolacz, J., L. P. Dale, E. J. Nix, O. K. Roath, G. F. Lewis, and S. W. Porges. 2020. "Adversity History Predicts Self-Reported Autonomic Reactivity and Mental Health in US Residents During the COVID-19 Pandemic." *Frontiers in Psychiatry* 11: 577728.

König, N., S. Steber, J. Seebacher, Q. von Prittwitz, H. R. Bliem, and S. Rossi. 2019. "How Therapeutic Tapping Can Alter Neural Correlates of Emotional Prosody Processing in Anxiety." *Brain Sciences* 9: 206.

Korn, D. L., and A. M. Leeds. 2002. "Preliminary Evidence of Efficacy for EMDR Resource Development and Installation in the Stabilization Phase of Treatment of Complex Posttraumatic Stress Disorder." *Journal of Clinical Psychology* 58: 1465–1487.

Kumari, M., and H. Karunaratne. 2022. "Therapeutic Effects of Yoga Nidra: A Review." *International Journal of Health Sciences and Research* 12: 148–153.

Laborde, S., M. Iskra, N. Zammit, U. Borges, M. You, C. Sevoz-Couche, and F. Dosseville. 2021. "Slow-Paced Breathing: Influence of Inhalation/Exhalation Ratio and of Respiratory Pauses on Cardiac Vagal Activity." *Sustainability* 13: 7775.

Lahl, O., C. Wispel, B. Willigens, and R. Pietrowsky. 2008. "An Ultra Short Episode of Sleep Is Sufficient to Promote Declarative Memory Performance." *Journal of Sleep Research* 17: 3–10.

Lanius, U. F., S. L. Paulsen, and F. M. Corrigan. 2014. *Neurobiology and the Treatment of Traumatic Dissociation: Towards an Embodied Self.* New York: Springer.

Levine, P. 2010. *In an Unspoken Voice: How the Body Releases Trauma and Restores Goodness.* Berkeley, CA: North Atlantic Books.

Mailk, S., I. Sarwar, K. N. Satti, and M. Jadoon. 2018. "The Frequency of Reversion of Paroxysmal Supra-Ventricular Tachycardia with Valsalva Maneuver." *Pakistan Journal of Surgery* 34: 219–223.

Magnon, V., F. Dutheil, and G. T. Vallet. 2021. "Benefits from One Session of Deep and Slow Breathing on Vagal Tone and Anxiety in Young and Older Adults." *Scientific Reports* 11: 19267.

Mantua, J., and R. M. C. Spencer. 2017. "Exploring the Nap Paradox: Are Mid-Day Sleep Bouts a Friend or Foe?" *Sleep Medicine* 37: 88–97.

Martins, D. F., F. J. F. Viseux, D. C. Salm, A. C. A. Ribeiro, H. K. L. da Silva, L. A. Seim, et al. 2021. "The Role of the Vagus Nerve in Fibromyalgia Syndrome." *Neuroscience and Biobehavioral Reviews* 131: 1136–1149.

McCraty, R., and D. Childre. 2010. "Coherence: Bridging Personal, Social, and Global Health." *Alternative Therapies in Health and Medicine* 16: 10–24.

McCraty, R., and M. A. Zayas. 2014. "Cardiac Coherence, Self-Regulation, Autonomic Stability, and Psychosocial Well-Being." *Frontiers in Psychology* 5: 1090.

McGilchrist, I. 2009. *The Master and His Emissary: The Divided Brain and the Making of the Western World*. New Haven, CT: Yale University Press.

Mednick, S. C., and M. Ehrman. 2006. *Take a Nap!: Change Your Life*. New York: Workman Publishing.

Meier, M., E. Unternaehrer, S. J. Dimitroff, A. B. E. Benz, U. U. Bentele, S. M. Schorpp, M. Wenzel, and J. C. Pruessner. 2020. "Standardized Massage Interventions as Protocols for the Induction of Psychophysiological Relaxation in the Laboratory: A Block Randomized, Controlled Trial." *Scientific Reports* 10: 14774.

Miller, J. 2023. *Body by Breath: The Science and Practice of Physical and Emotional Resilience*. Las Vegas: Victory Belt Publishing.

Molero-Chamizo, A., M. A. Nitsche, A. Bolz, R. T. Andújar Barroso, J. R. Alameda Bailén, J. C. García Palomeque, and G. N. Rivera-Urbina. 2022. "Non-Invasive Transcutaneous

Vagus Nerve Stimulation for the Treatment of Fibromyalgia Symptoms: A Study Protocol." *Brain Sciences* 12: 95.

Mondal, S. 2024. "Proposed Physiological Mechanisms of Pranayama: A Discussion." *Journal of Ayurveda and Integrative Medicine* 15: 100877.

Niazi, I. K., M. S. Navid, J. Bartley, D. Shepherd, M. Pedersen, G. Burns, D. Taylor, and D. E. White. 2022. "EEG Signatures Change During Unilateral Yogi Nasal Breathing." *Scientific Reports* 12: 520.

Ogden, P., and J. Fisher. 2015. *Sensorimotor Psychotherapy: Interventions for Trauma and Attachment.* New York: W. W. Norton.

Pagaduan, J., S. S. Wu, T. Kameneva, and E. Lambert. 2019. "Acute Effects of Resonance Frequency Breathing on Cardiovascular Regulation." *Physiological Reports* 7: E14295.

Pagani, M., G. Di Lorenzo, A. R. Verardo, G. Nicolais, L. Monaco, G. Lauretti, et al. 2012. "Neurobiological Correlates of EMDR Monitoring: An EEG Study." *PLoS ONE* 7: E45753.

Pandi-Perumal, S. R., D. W. Spence, N. Srivastava, D. Kanchibhotla, K. Kumar, G. S. Sharma, R. Gupta, and G. Batmanabane. 2022. "The Origin and Clinical Relevance of Yoga Nidra." *Sleep and Vigilance* 6: 61–84.

Pang, A. S. K. 2016. *Rest: Why You Get More Done When You Work Less.* New York: Basic Books.

Pert, C. B. 1997. *Molecules of Emotion: Why You Feel the Way You Feel.* New York: Scribner.

Parnell, L. 2008. *Tapping In: A Step-by-Step Guide to Activating Your Healing Resources Through Bilateral Stimulation.* Boulder, CO: Sounds True.

Phillips, W. J., and D. W. Hine. 2021. "Self-Compassion, Physical Health, and Health Behaviour: A Meta-Analysis." *Health Psychology Review* 15: 113–139.

Porges, S. W. 2004. "Neuroception: A Subconscious System for Detecting Threats and Safety." *Zero to Three* 24: 19–24.

———. 2011. *The Polyvagal Theory: Neurophysiological Foundations of Emotions, Attachment, Communication, and Self-Regulation.* New York: W. W. Norton.

————. 2017. *The Pocket Guide to the Polyvagal Theory: The Transformative Power of Feeling Safe*. New York: W. W. Norton.

Porges, S. W., and G. F. Lewis. 2010. "The Polyvagal Hypothesis: Common Mechanisms Mediating Autonomic Regulation, Vocalizations and Listening." In *Handbook of Mammalian Vocalization: An Integrative Neuroscience Approach*, edited by S. M. Bruzynski. Burlington, MA: Academic Press.

Ramkissoon, C. M., A. Güemes, and J. Vehi. 2021. "Overview of Therapeutic Applications of Non-invasive Vagus Nerve Stimulation: A Motivation for Novel Treatments for Systemic Lupus Erythematosus." *Bioelectronic Medicine* 7: 8.

Rasmussen, S. E., M. Pfeiffer-Jensen, A. M. Drewes, A. D. Farmer, B. W. Deleuran, K. Stengaard-Pedersen, B. Brock, and C. Brock. 2018. "Vagal Influences in Rheumatoid Arthritis." *Scandinavian Journal of Rheumatology* 47: 1–11.

Rattaz, V., N. Puglisi, H. Tissot, and N. Favez. 2022. "Associations Between Parent–Infant Interactions, Cortisol and Vagal Regulation in Infants, and Socioemotional Outcomes: A Systematic Review." *Infant Behavior and Development* 67: 101687.

Rinne-Albers, M. A. W., S. J. A. van der Werff, M. J. van Hoof, N. D. van Lang, F. Lamers-Winkelman, S. A. Rombouts, R. R. J. M. Vermeiren, and N. J. A. van der Wee. 2016. "Abnormalities of White Matter Integrity in the Corpus Callosum of Adolescents with PTSD After Childhood Sexual Abuse: A DTI Study." *European Child and Adolescent Psychiatry* 25: 869–878.

Russell, M. E. B., A. B. Scott, I. A. Boggero, and C. R. Carlson. 2017. "Inclusion of a Rest Period in Diaphragmatic Breathing Increases High Frequency Heart Rate Variability: Implications for Behavioral Therapy." *Psychophysiology* 54: 358–365.

Ruden, R. A. 2005. "A Neurological Basis for the Observed Peripheral Sensory Modulation of Emotional Responses." *Traumatology* 11: 145–158.

————. 2019. "Harnessing Electroceuticals to Treat Disorders Arising from Traumatic Stress: Theoretical Considerations Using a Psychosensory Model." *Explore* 15: 222–229.

Scaer, R. 2014. *The Body Bears the Burden: Trauma, Dissociation, and Disease*, 3rd ed. New York: Routledge.

Schirmer, A., I. Croy, and R. Ackerley. 2023. "What Are C-Tactile Afferents and How Do They Relate to 'Affective Touch'?" *Neuroscience and Biobehavioral Reviews* 151: 105236.

Schleip, R. 2017. "Fascia as a Sensory Organ: Clinical Applications." *Terra Rosa E-Mag* 20: 2–7.

Schore, A. N. 2019. *Right Brain Psychotherapy*. New York: W. W. Norton.

Siegel, D. 1999. *The Developing Mind: How Relationships and the Brain Interact to Shape Who We Are*. New York: Guilford.

———. 2010. *Mindsight: The New Science of Personal Transformation*. New York: Bantam.

Stankovic, L. 2011. "Transforming Trauma: A Qualitative Feasibility Study of Integrative Restoration (iRest) Yoga Nidra on Combat-Related Post-Traumatic Stress Disorder." *International Journal of Yoga Therapy* 21: 23–37.

Stickgold, R. 2002. "EMDR: A Putative Neurobiological Mechanism of Action." *Journal of Clinical Psychology*, 58, 61–75.

Tanaka-Arakawa, M. M., M. Matsui, C. Tanaka, A. Uematsu, S. Uda, K. Miura, T. Sakai, and K. Noguchi. 2015. "Developmental Changes in the Corpus Callosum from Infancy to Early Adulthood: A Structural Magnetic Resonance Imaging Study." *PLoS ONE* 10: e0118760.

Telles, S., M. Singh, and A. Balkrishna. 2011. "Heart rate variability changes during high frequency yoga breathing and breath awareness." *Biopsychosocial Medicine* 5: 4.

Telles, S., S. Verma, S. K. Sharma, R. K. Gupta, and A. Balkrishna. 2017. "Alternate-Nostril Yoga Breathing Reduced Blood Pressure While Increasing Performance in a Vigilance Test." *Medical Science Monitor Basic Research* 23: 392–398.

Thomson, P. 2007. "'Down Will Come Baby': Prenatal Stress, Primitive Defenses, and Gestational Dysregulation." *Journal of Trauma and Dissociation* 8: 85–113.

Trakroo, M., and A. B. Bhavanani. 2016. "Physiological Benefits of Yogic Practices: A Brief Review." *International Journal of Traditional and Complementary Medicine* 1: 0031–0043.

Treleaven, D. A. 2018. *Trauma-Sensitive Mindfulness: Practices for Safe and Transformative Healing*. New York: W. W. Norton.

Truitt, K. 2022. *Healing in Your Hands: Self-Havening Practices to Harness Neuroplasticity, Heal Traumatic Stress, and Build Resilience.* Eau Claire, WI: PESI Publishing.

Walker, P. 2013. *Complex PTSD: From Surviving to Thriving: A Guide and Map for Recovering from Childhood Trauma.* Lafayette, CA: Azure Coyote.

Wesarg, C., A. L. Van den Akker, N. Y. L. Oei, R. W. Wiers, J. Staaks, J. F. Thayer, D. P. Williams, and M. Hoeve. 2022. "Childhood Adversity and Vagal Regulation: A Systematic Review and Meta-Analysis." *Neuroscience and Biobehavioral Reviews* 143: 104920.

Woo, M. S., M. Shafiq, A. Fitzek, M. Dottermusch, H. Altmeppen, B. Mohammadi, et al. 2023. "Vagus Nerve Inflammation Contributes to Dysautonomia in COVID-19." *Acta Neuropathologica* 146: 387–394.

Wright, K. P., A. W. McHill, B. R. Birks, B. R. Griffin, T. Rusterholz, and E. D. Chinoy. 2013. "Entrainment of the Human Circadian Clock to the Natural Light-Dark Cycle." *Current Biology* 23: 1554–1558.

Zou, L., J. E. Sasaki, G.-X. Wei, T. Huang, A. S. Yeung, O. B. Neto, K. W. Chen, and S. S.-C. Hui. 2018. "Effects of Mind–Body Exercises (Tai Chi/Yoga) on Heart Rate Variability Parameters and Perceived Stress: A Systematic Review with Meta-Analysis of Randomized Controlled Trials." *Journal of Clinical Medicine* 7: 404.

Arielle Schwartz, PhD, is a licensed clinical psychologist, certified complex trauma professional, eye movement desensitization and reprocessing (EMDR) consultant, and Kripalu yoga teacher. She is an internationally sought-out speaker, leading voice in the field of trauma recovery, and award-winning author. As a faculty member at the Polyvagal Institute, she is a course instructor on mind-body approaches that apply polyvagal theory for trauma recovery. She earned her doctorate in clinical psychology at Fielding Graduate University, and holds a master's degree in somatic psychology through Naropa University. She is author of seven books, including *The Complex PTSD Workbook, EMDR Therapy and Somatic Psychology*, and *The Post-Traumatic Growth Guidebook*.

Foreword writer **Linda Thai, LMSW**, is a trauma therapist who specializes in complex developmental trauma. Born in Vietnam, raised in Australia, and now living in Alaska, she is a former child refugee who is passionate about breaking the cycle of historical and intergenerational trauma at individual and community levels.

Real change *is* possible

For more than fifty years, New Harbinger has published
proven-effective self-help books and pioneering
workbooks to help readers of all ages and backgrounds
improve mental health and well-being, and achieve lasting
personal growth. In addition, our spirituality books
offer profound guidance for deepening awareness and
cultivating healing, self-discovery, and fulfillment.

Founded by psychologist Matthew McKay and
Patrick Fanning, New Harbinger is proud to be
an independent, employee-owned company.
Our books reflect our core values of integrity, innovation,
commitment, sustainability, compassion, and trust.
Written by leaders in the field and recommended by
therapists worldwide, New Harbinger books are practical,
accessible, and provide real tools for real change.

 **newharbinger**publications

MORE BOOKS from
NEW HARBINGER PUBLICATIONS

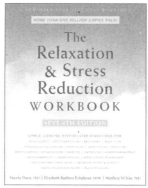

Did you know there are **free tools** you can download for this book?

Free tools are things like **worksheets, guided meditation exercises**, and **more** that will help you get the most out of your book.

You can download free tools for this book— whether you bought or borrowed it, in any format, from any source—from the New Harbinger website. All you need is a NewHarbinger.com account. Just use the URL provided in this book to view the free tools that are available for it. Then, click on the "download" button for the free tool you want, and follow the prompts that appear to log in to your NewHarbinger.com account and download the material.

You can also save the free tools for this book to your **Free Tools Library** so you can access them again anytime, just by logging in to your account! Just look for this button on the book's free tools page.

+ Save this to my free tools library